Endorsements

"Caregiving is a selfless and demanding call that will be deserving of significant rewards in Heaven. I am a caregiver for a loved one, and I realize very well the energy, emotion, and time required to tend well to the needs of the one you are called to serve. Caregivers are often overlooked, but they need to be supported, encouraged, and invested into.

Darlene Goodwin's 31-day devotional for caregivers, *Keeping Mother*, is a valuable support instrument that will refresh and empower all who serve and minister in a caregiving capacity. Well done, Darlene, and thank you!"

—Patricia King
Author, Minister, Media Host, and Producer

"If you are a caregiver, this book is for you! As Christ followers, we have the privilege and responsibility to show and share His love with those around us. We are especially entrusted with the care of our own family members, and in *Keeping Mother: A 31-Day Devotional for Caregivers*, Darlene Goodwin gives us the daily doses of encouragement and biblical guidance we need for giving care that is empowered by God's Spirit and His grace. Without Him, we can do nothing! But with Christ's power infusing us, we can love beyond limits and give the excellent care that honors and glorifies God and ministers His life and peace to those whom we 'keep.'

One thing is certain, when you are a giver, you need refilling. Let this book be a source of refreshment to your soul as you serve Christ by serving others."

—Teresa Yancy
Cofounder, Unlocking Your Book
Author, *Unveiled by God*

"Dear readers, if you are embarking on the journey of taking care of your loved one with dementia, then you take on a monumental task of love. After watching Darlene walk this journey day in and day out, I believe you can trust the solid biblical principles that she lays out to help you through all the mountains and valleys of caregiving."

—Chaplain Nikki Weikel
MDiv

"As the owner and executive director of a senior home care agency, our daily mission is to help people care for their loved ones. I've experienced families dedicating their love, time, and resources to supporting a parent in need of care. It's a labor of love I learned first-hand as a caregiver for both my mother and my mother-in-law. Unfortunately, for many, the labor quickly overwhelms the love from which it is given. Through the years, I've seen families come together and get torn apart. The physical and emotional struggle that senior care, especially with a parent suffering with dementia, places on a family caregiver can become overwhelming at times. The common pattern for those who succeed? Faith in God and an unswaying love for a parent—the two themes of Darlene Goodwin's book, *Keeping Mother: A 31-Day Devotional for Caregivers.*

I was blessed to watch firsthand as she fought through the difficult labor of being a caregiver to honor the love she had for God and her mother. I recognized many of the events she describes in *Keeping Mother* and witnessed how Darlene's incredible faith helped her overcome the challenges of taking care of a parent suffering with dementia. It was inspirational for me as well as all our caregivers who came into her home. Quite often, we look back to those lessons when we face our own struggles and successes as a company. Thankfully, Darlene shares many of those experiences in her devotional. It outlines her struggles and how her faith helped to overcome those difficulties. It's a spiritually-grounded roadmap to help navigate the arduous job of caregiving for a loved one suffering with dementia.

God led my wife and me to start our home care company as a ministry. He asked us to use our experience as caregivers with our parents to help others. Darlene does the same in her devotional. She blessed us as we watched her care for her mother. Her devotional will similarly bless the reader."

—Dean Longo
Owner, Visiting Angels of Norfolk Virginia

Keeping Mother

Keeping Mother

A 31-Day Devotional for Caregivers

Copyright © 2023 by Darlene Goodwin

All rights reserved.

No part of this book may be reproduced in any form or by any electronic or mechanical means, including information storage and retrieval systems, without written permission from the author, except for the use of brief quotations in a book review.

Scripture quotations marked TPT are from The Passion Translation®. Copyright © 2017, 2018, 2020 by Passion & Fire Ministries, Inc. Scripture quotations marked (NKJV) are taken from the New King James Version®. Copyright © 1982 by Thomas Nelson. Used by permission. All rights reserved.

ISBN Paperback: 978-1-961557-62-8

ISBN Ebook: 978-1-961557-63-5

ISBN Hardback: 978-1-961557-91-8

Library of Congress Control Number: 9781961557628

Published in 2024.

Messenger Books
30 N. Gould Ste. R
Sheridan, WY 82801

Dedication

*To my Lord and Savior, Jesus Christ, with profound
gratitude for His immense love and grace.
May this devotional draw each reader closer to
Him and bring Him honor.*

*To my parents, now with the Lord,
with my deepest love and respect:
My earthly father, Kimble, for his wonderful and bountiful
provision of fatherly love, enabling me to readily and
joyfully receive divine love from my Heavenly Father.*

*My mother, Phyllis, a caregiver by divine design who
exemplified selfless love, mercy, and grace. I pray this book
will honor her memory and infuse every reader with
courage to care for loved ones in the same manner that she
did—with steadfast devotion and faithfulness.*

Contents

Endorsements	1
Dedication	9
Foreword	13
Introduction	15
An Invitation: Do You Know Jesus?	19
Day 1—Behold Your Mother!	23

Part One
Abiding

Day 2—Abide in the Vine	29
Day 3—Hearing His Voice	33
Day 4—Your Divine Teacher and Encourager	37
Day 5—With Him, All Things Are Possible	41
Day 6—Perfectly Peaceful	45

Part Two
Serving

Day 7—Becoming a Servant	51
Day 8—His Command to Love	55
Day 9—Giving Honor	59
Day 10—Perseverance for the Journey	64
Day 11—As Unto Him	68

Part Three
Believing

Day 12—Faith That Pleases God	75
Day 13—Your Words Declare	79
Day 14—Think on These Things	83
Day 15—Stand, Therefore	88
Day 16—Choose Joy	92

Part Four
Living

Day 17—Your Story, Written in Heaven	99
Day 18—Live in His Blessing	103
Day 19—His Victory Is Yours	107
Day 20—Prosper in Covenant	111
Day 21—Divine Health	115

Part Five
Giving

Day 22—Sowing and Reaping	121
Day 23—Give	125
Day 24—The Gift of Forgiveness	129
Day 25—Be a Wonder-Worker: Encourage	134
Day 26—Cast Vision	138

Part Six
Shining

Day 27—Gaze Upon Him and Shine	145
Day 28—Reflect the Fruit of the Spirit	149
Day 29—Seek Divine Appointments—and Be One	154
Day 30—Walking Homeward	159
Day 31—Letting Go and Going Forth	163

Resources for Growing in Christ	167
Notes	169
Acknowledgments	171
Letter from the Author	173
About the Author	175

Foreword

The book you hold in your hand is not only a poignant tribute to the author's journey but also a guiding light for anyone who finds themselves in the role of caregiver, facing the challenges and demands of caring for a loved one in their time of greatest need. *Keeping Mother* is more than just a book; it is a profound testament to the enduring power of love, faith, and the incredible strength of the human spirit.

Darlene Goodwin's personal story of being a caregiver for her elderly mother during an eleven-year battle with dementia and cancer is both touching and inspiring. She takes us on a deeply emotional journey, sharing glimpses of the heartrending experiences that caregivers often face, the triumphs and the tribulations, and the unwavering dedication to their loved ones.

One of the most powerful aspects of this book is its focus on the role of faith in the caregiving journey. Darlene beautifully illustrates how faith can be a source of unyielding strength, providing solace and guidance in the most challenging of circumstances. Through her daily devotions, we are offered meaningful reflections, prayers, and words of wisdom that not only provide comfort but also instill a sense of hope and purpose in the caregiver's heart.

Keeping Mother serves as a believer's guide to the essential qualities needed in the caregiving role: patience, compassion, resilience, and, most importantly, love. Darlene's love for her mother and her steadfast belief in God's mercy and grace serve as a beacon of inspiration for us all. Her devotions will undoubtedly touch the hearts of caregivers, reminding them that they are not alone in their journey and that a tenderhearted Father is watching over them.

In a world where caregiving can often feel isolating and overwhelming, this devotional offers a sense of community and a reservoir of spiritual support. It is a book that not only provides valuable insights into the practical aspects of caregiving but also nourishes the soul. I wholeheartedly recommend this book to anyone who is a caregiver or knows someone in that role. It will leave an indelible mark on your heart and soul. Darlene Goodwin's *Keeping Mother* is a true gift to caregivers and their loved ones, reminding us all that in the darkest moments, the light of faith can guide us through.

Brian Simmons
Passion & Fire Ministries

Introduction

"Let us therefore come boldly to the throne of grace, that we may obtain mercy and find grace to help in time of need."

— Hebrews 4:16, NKJV

Keeping Mother is my story about the sufficiency of God's mercy and grace that carried a daughter through her time of greatest need—the sudden, unforeseen season of caring for her elderly mother at home through an eleven-year battle with dementia and cancer.

Though I had never considered myself the caregiver type, as Mother's only living child, the responsibility for her care became mine to steward. It stretched me in ways I could not have imagined and demanded more than I had to give, but with the Lord's help, I was able to grant Mother's desire to be home with me in her final years until she went to her heavenly home.

Life had been going along well. I was grateful for the blessings of a lovely home in a bayside community, a wonderful church, career satisfaction, and supportive friends and family. Dad had gone to be with the Lord years earlier, so I had brought Mother to live nearby. Her welfare was my priority as her only daughter. I wanted to remain close during her senior years and help her as needed.

I was not prepared for what was to come.

Reflecting back, I see the Lord's hand in bringing family caregivers into my path during the decades leading up to my own caregiving season. I found myself deeply respectful of these people who willingly sacrificed so much, setting their own life plans aside to care for their loved one at home.

Despite my admiration for their service, I wasn't sure I had the personal fortitude to make such a profound commitment. Oh, I loved my mother! I just figured I would be *overseeing* any needed care…not *providing* it. I didn't feel qualified or adept at that kind of thing. Mother had been a caregiver—not me!

Then one day, my moment of decision arrived.

I had a choice to make. Mother could no longer live on her own, and the responsibility to choose her future home now rested upon me.

I didn't know the way forward, but I knew the One who did. And, somehow, I knew the answer… Mother's place was with me. Thankfully, I wasn't aware of what the coming years would hold (and, likely, could not have comprehended it). But I knew God's grace would be more than sufficient, as it was.

Today, with that season passed, I am ever-so-grateful for my choice. Though it was clearly not the easy path, keeping Mother at home for those years yielded abundant heavenly rewards that enriched our lives in ways that, I'm quite sure, nothing else could have.

Most importantly, it was best for her!

Second only to receiving Jesus as my Savior, I believe that keeping Mother was the most significant and important decision I've ever made. Yet, I am convinced, had it not been for the Lord's continual provision of grace and mercy, I could not have persevered through such a prolonged season of intense challenge.

To be clear, it was a wonderful blessing to have Mother with me, but the unwelcome intruder of disease that attacked her mind and body complicated life in unpleasant ways for both of us. The onslaught, beyond her ability to control, caused her to behave, at times, unlike her normal self and hindered my best efforts to assist her.

Through it all, the Lord remained our Ever-Present Help.

My journals from that season reveal what often inspired me —the devotional I had read that day! Like searching for hidden treasure, I anticipated reading the perfectly portioned, power-packed message-of-the-day to see how the Lord would personalize it for me.

Often exceeding my expectations, He frequently expounded upon the text in ways I'm quite sure the author could never have imagined. You see, He had already made provision for what He knew I would need that day.

If today, you're "keeping" your own loved one and yearning for that deeper connection with the Lord for supernatural strength, this devotional has been affectionately penned with you in mind.

A dear friend prayed with me that the Father would bless the words I write to flow from His heart, through mine, to yours. I trust He heard our prayer.

> *"Since we have this confidence, we can also have great boldness before him, for if we ask anything agreeable to his will, he will hear us. And if we know that he hears us in whatever we ask, we also know that we have obtained the requests we ask of him."*
>
> — 1 John 5:14–15, TPT

May the Lord's joy be your strength as He leads you in your devoted service, and may you discover throughout these pages valuable nuggets of treasure personally crafted for you from your Father's heart.

An Invitation: Do You Know Jesus?

"For this is how much God loved the world—he gave his one and only, unique Son as a gift. So now everyone who believes in him will never perish but experience everlasting life. God did not send his Son into the world to judge and condemn the world, but to be its Savior and rescue it!"

— John 3:16–17, TPT

Congratulations! I've saved the best for first, and you're about to read the most important message of this book. It's where I reveal the number one Gift I can offer to every reader, whether or not you're caring for a loved one. In fact, nothing else I could ever share even comes close.

According to God's Word, this Gift provides you with free and forever access to:

- Having your sins paid for—in full (Ephesians 1:7).

- Supernatural peace (John 14:27), healing (1 Peter 2:24), protection (Psalm 91), and blessings (Ephesians 1:3).
- Provision of supply for your every need (Philippians 4:19) by the One who can do immeasurably more than *all* you could ever ask or imagine (Ephesians 3:20).
- Eternal life (1 John 2:25).
- And much, much more (1 Corinthians 2:9).

Jesus is the Gift, and I would like to invite you into a deeper relationship with Him. He loves you with an everlasting love and offers life more abundantly (John 10:10).

We all need a Savior. According to Romans 3:23 and 6:23, all have sinned—and the wages of sin is death—but the gift of God is eternal life in Christ Jesus. Those who receive Him by faith are justified by His grace and empowered to live free of condemnation as they walk according to the Spirit (Romans 8:1).

The Bible is clear—Jesus is the only way of salvation. As we read in Acts 4:12 (NKJV), *"Nor is there salvation in any other, for there is no other name under heaven given among men by which we must be saved."* In John 14:6, Jesus said, *"I am the way, the truth, and the life. No one comes to the Father except through Me."* His blood, alone, atones for our sin (1 John 1:7).

Perhaps you have already received this Gift, and if so, cherish Him as the Gift that keeps giving! If you have not yet received this Gift and desire to invite Jesus into your heart to be your Savior, ask Him now. Here is a Scripture and prayer to guide you:

> *"If you confess with your mouth the Lord Jesus and believe in your heart that God has raised Him from the dead, you will be saved. For with the heart one believes unto righteousness, and with the mouth confession is made unto salvation."*
>
> — ROMANS 10:9–10, NKJV

Pray this:

> "Lord Jesus, I confess that I have sinned and am in need of Your forgiveness and grace. I believe in my heart and confess with my mouth that You are Lord, and I now receive You as my Savior and the Lord of my life. Thank you for redeeming me with Your precious blood and for Your gift of salvation!"

If you prayed that prayer, there is rejoicing in Heaven for you today!

You are embarking on a wonderful adventure of faith! I can testify after nearly fifty years of walking with Jesus—the journey gets sweeter as the days go by, and the blessing of receiving a continual flow of rich insight from His Word is delightful beyond measure.

At the back of this book, I have provided a list of a few helpful resources to guide you in your new walk with Christ.

MY PRAYER FOR YOU

> *Heavenly Father, I thank You for each person reading these pages. May Your joy be their strength, Your*

Word their guiding light, and Your grace their comfort, all the days of their lives. For each one who prays the prayer of salvation, keep them in Your tender care. Help them to fully activate the faith You have given, and to shine their light so brightly that others will see Your brilliance reflected in them and desire closeness with You. To Your glory!

In the name of Jesus, I pray. Amen.

Day 1—Behold Your Mother!

"Now there stood by the cross of Jesus His mother, and His mother's sister ... and Mary Magdalene. When Jesus therefore saw His mother, and the disciple whom He loved standing by, He said to His mother, 'Woman, behold your son!' Then He said to the disciple, 'Behold your mother!' And from that hour that disciple took her to his own home."

— John 19:25–27, NKJV

Have you ever considered what a precious gift you are to the one you care for?

Caring for an elderly loved one at home is a beautiful example of Christlikeness in that we choose to devote our lives to help another in great need. But sacrificing our own desires and life plans is rarely an easy choice. The challenges that accompany a caregiving season are often overwhelming, so much so that we can become weary in well doing, even to the point of wanting to give up.

Always remember that through it all and despite any circumstance, your decision each day to serve your loved one retains enduring, and even eternal, significance.

Consider the words of Jesus from the cross. In one of His final utterances before His death, our Savior boldly declared provision of a son, His disciple John, to care for His mother, Mary.

Why this dying act from the cross?

We know from Scripture that Jesus was aware of the approaching time for His sacrificial death (Matthew 26:2). Surely, had it been His desire, He could have chosen a private conversation beforehand with John about His mother. But for reasons we can only surmise, the Lord chose a public declaration of provision for His mother—from the cross.

The words of Christ carry a unique magnitude through time and eternity. He *is* the Word of life (1 John 1:1), and His words will by no means pass away (Mark 13:31). Jesus' words spoken from the cross include some of the most well-known phrases in the Bible:

- "Father, forgive them, for they know not what they do,"
- "Assuredly I say to you, today you will be with Me in paradise,"
- "My God, My God, Why have You forsaken Me?"
- and the pronouncement of His completed work of redemption, "It is finished!"

Perhaps not as widely recognized as the other sayings of Jesus from the cross, His declaration entrusting Mary into

John's care holds its own significance, highlighting His attentiveness to His mother's well-being *in the very moments* He was bearing the sins of the world.

Though we can't presume to fully understand the Lord's motivation for this public act at such a pivotal moment in history, or why He chose His friend and apostle, John, to care for Mary—His actions indicate He wanted it known…a lesson in love for us all. Love provides, and He is Love.

Jesus said, *"I do nothing of Myself; but as My Father taught Me, I speak these things"* (John 8:28). How beautiful to consider that Jesus' thoughtful gift to Mary actually originated from the heart of God the Father.

As for John, his response to this presumably unexpected assignment was immediate obedience to the Lord. We read in the Scriptures that he took Mary to his home *from that hour*. John accepted full responsibility for her current and future needs by receiving her as his own mother.

Was your assumption of caregiving duties abrupt? Unexpected? If so, you're not alone. Often, family caregivers find their lives suddenly interrupted and priorities shifted when a loved one becomes unable to live independently.

Though your opportunity to care may not have come at a convenient time, you made the choice to do so. You chose love. It may cost you dearly—in your daily routine, relationships with other family members, your finances, your career. Our God is a Redeemer, and you can surrender all of these things into His capable hands. Your decision to care reveals a reflection of Jesus in you as you give precedence to your dear one, just when they need you the most.

Such a priceless gift of love! Much like the one Jesus—and John—gave Mary.

Reflection and Application

As you consider the significance of the Lord's provision for His mother from the cross, how does this affect your feelings about the importance of caring for your loved one?

In what ways does the emphasis Jesus placed on Mary's well-being help you to persevere in your dedication to your loved one through the challenges that come with caregiving?

John responded to Jesus in obedience, taking Mary to his home as his mother. What has the Lord asked of you that is requiring your obedience? Identify any hindrances to obeying His Word, and ask Him for help to accomplish all He has called you to do this day.

Prayer of Declaration

> *Heavenly Father, just as Jesus showed His love for Mary by providing for her from the cross, and John was obedient to receive and serve her as his own mother, I dedicate myself to loving and providing for my dear one with greater devotion. Thank You for strengthening me for the journey. May my service to them, given as unto You, demonstrate Your love to them, and may my every thought, word, and deed bring You honor and glory. In the name of Jesus, I pray. Amen.*

Part One

Abiding

"Abide in Me, and I in you. As the branch cannot bear fruit of itself, unless it abides in the vine, neither can you, unless you abide in Me."

— John 15:4, NKJV

Day 2—Abide in the Vine

"I am the vine, you are the branches. He who abides in Me, and I in him, bears much fruit; for without Me you can do nothing. ... If you abide in Me, and My words abide in you, you will ask what you desire, and it shall be done for you. By this My Father is glorified, that you bear much fruit."

— John 15:5, 7–8, NKJV

Without Jesus, we can do nothing. With Him, all things are possible! The extent to which we abide in Him impacts everything else in our lives. Our obedience to abide, and to allow ourselves to be filled with His Word, opens the door to His promises: that we will bear much fruit and that we may ask what we desire, believing that it will be done. And in these things, the Father will be glorified!

Learning to abide in Jesus is an important key that unlocks our ability to consistently walk in victory over challenging circumstances. It takes perseverance and focus. Our spirit is willing, but our flesh is weak, and our adversary often employs the tactic of distraction against us. We must remain vigilant and resist his efforts to deflect our focus from the very thing that will garner our victory. James 4:7 instructs us to submit ourselves to God, resist the devil, and he will flee. Our ability to declare and stand on God's Word is a mighty weapon in spiritual warfare!

How do we know if we're abiding in the Lord? His Word tells us. Note the various aspects of abiding recorded in 1 John 4:12–16 (NKJV):

- If we love one another, God abides in us.
- By this, we know that we abide in Him, and He in us, because He has given us His Spirit.
- Whoever confesses that Jesus is the Son of God, God abides in him, and he in God.
- God is love. He who abides in love abides in God, and God in him.

Our part? Love. And confess Jesus as Lord.

God's part? He *is* love, and He *has given* us His Spirit. He offers us such good gifts—should we not fully take hold of them?

Practically speaking, an important aspect of abiding is waiting on the Lord, though waiting and abiding do have distinctions:

- Waiting on the Lord can take various forms but is often accomplished during a period of time in prayer

as we pause quietly before Him, meditate on His Word, and position ourselves to hear His voice.
- Abiding infers a constant state of being. We can abide in the Lord every moment of every day, whether at rest or active.

This is good news for the busy caregiver!

You may be wondering how you can take time to abide in the Lord when you're already feeling overwhelmed or burdened. Remember that you can always abide in Jesus, regardless of what else you are having to attend to (and, while you're there, cast your care on Him to lighten your load). Be encouraged that even a few moments of drawing near to the Lord can produce benefits. I challenge you to give it a try! I believe you will find daily tasks much more manageable and an enhanced ability to maintain a pleasant disposition, even amidst difficulties.

As you abide in Jesus, draw deeply and consistently from the well of living water that flows freely. There, in that secret place hidden with the Lover of your soul, you will discover a supernatural spring of spiritual hydration—as essential to abundant life as water is to your physical body. As you are refreshed with this living water, your caregiving duties can be embraced as opportunities to joyfully serve your dear one, rather than burdensome tasks you take on with resentment and irritation.

Abide in the Vine. Time spent abiding in Him and waiting on Him will always be a wellspring of blessing for you. And as you are filled with living water, you become a spring from which others are refreshed!

Reflection and Application

Think about one or two individuals who, in your observation, have mastered the ability to abide in the Lord. What attributes do they display that are consistent with abiding in Jesus, and what fruit do you see being produced in their lives?

Prayerfully consider how you can more fully abide in Jesus. Identify one change you can make to your daily schedule to prioritize a devoted focus on Him.

Throughout your waking hours, become aware of abiding in Him in every circumstance and look for evidence of His Presence. As you abide in Him, know that He abides in you!

Prayer of Declaration

*Heavenly Father, Your Word says that when I abide in Jesus and He in me, I will bear much fruit that will bring glory to You. Teach me to abide in Jesus.
I desire to please You and bear much fruit for You.
As I abide, make me a spring of Your living water to refresh those around me.
In the name of Jesus, I pray. Amen.*

Day 3—Hearing His Voice

"And the sheep recognize the voice of the true Shepherd, for he calls his own by name and leads them out, for they belong to him. And when he has brought out all his sheep, he walks ahead of them and they will follow him, for they are familiar with his voice. But they will run away from strangers and never follow them because they know it's the voice of a stranger."

— John 10:3–5, TPT

As a new believer, I used to hear people say things like, "The Lord told me this," or "I heard the Lord say…" and I would wonder how they could hear from the Lord, how they distinguished His voice from their own thoughts.

I wanted to hear from Him; I just didn't know how. Nor did I realize that the Lord had given me a promise in Scripture: His sheep hear His voice! As a sheep knows and heeds the voice of its shepherd, the Lord had already placed in me an innate ability to communicate with Him as my True Shepherd and Heavenly Father.

Hearing the Lord speak wasn't something I had to strive to figure out how to do. It was as natural for me to have a relationship with my Father in Heaven as with my earthly father.

Some of you may recall life before caller ID and cell phones. When I was a teenager in the 1970s, we had a telephone on the wall in the kitchen, and there was another phone in my bedroom. If, for instance, I was talking to my grandmother on the phone in my room, my mother could have been on the phone in the kitchen joining in on the conversation.

When the phone would ring in those days, you just had to answer it to find out who was on the other end of the line—there were no displays on the phone with the name, number, or location of the caller.

One night, I had just gotten into a deep sleep when the phone rang. (Back then, there was also no turning off the ringer!) Still half asleep, I picked up the handset and answered. It was what we used to call a crank caller, and with no caller ID, there was no way of knowing who the caller was.

I remember struggling to wake up while trying to talk to the man and figure out what he was saying. Then, in an instant, my confusion was displaced by a deep sense of calm when I heard the voice of my father on the line. He had picked up the phone in the other room. He said firmly, "Darlene, hang up the phone!" And in my semi-conscious state, I instinctively obeyed, with no question or hesitation.

The moment he spoke, I recognized my father's voice and the inherent authority it carried—and I was comforted knowing that he would take care of the situation. I was free to simply go back to sleep.

How did I distinguish the sound of my father's voice from that of the crank caller? The voice of the caller was totally unfamiliar to me. I had no relationship with that man—he was a stranger to me.

I immediately knew my father's voice because I had been close with him all of my life. He was my protector and provider with whom I had established a deep level of trust. We had enjoyed many shared experiences. He was a good father, and as his daughter, I belonged to him. His voice was intimately familiar to me. Where he would lead, I would follow.

Much like the way my dad's voice soothed my emotions over the phone that night, the voice of our Heavenly Father calms us when we are distressed, reassures us and imparts courage when we feel fearful or uncertain, and conveys an authority like no other.

As His child, one of your greatest needs is to hear His voice.

As a caregiver, you may find yourself burdened by confounding situations, feeling exhausted and in need of guidance and help, unsure of where to turn. Take heart in the scriptural assurance that your Heavenly Father has answers that precede your questions and has made provision before your need becomes apparent. Give Him preeminence over everything else in life. Stand on His promises, and rest in your identity as His beloved child who hears His voice.

Reflection and Application

Prayerfully meditate on these Scriptures for insight into the Father's heart and His desire for you to hear His voice. Guided by these verses, draw close to Him…and listen!

- *"Look with wonder at the depth of the Father's marvelous love that he has lavished on us! He has called us and made us his very own beloved children"* (1 John 3:1, TPT).
- *"For it was always in his perfect plan to adopt us as his delightful children, through our union with Jesus, the Anointed One, so that his tremendous love that cascades over us would glorify his grace—for the same love he has for the Beloved, Jesus, he has for us"* (Ephesians 1:5–6, TPT).
- *"But He answered and said, 'It is written, "Man shall not live by bread alone, but by every word that proceeds from the mouth of God"'"* (Matthew 4:4, NKJV).
- *"And all these blessings shall come upon you and overtake you, because you obey the voice of the Lord your God"* (Deuteronomy 28:2, NKJV).

Prayer of Declaration

*Heavenly Father, thank You for making me
Your beloved child—and for assuring me in Your Word that
I hear Your voice. I will listen attentively
to hear You speak and I will joyfully obey,
as I draw closer to You day by day!
In the name of Jesus, I pray. Amen.*

Day 4—Your Divine Teacher and Encourager

> "But when the truth-giving Spirit comes, he will unveil the reality of every truth within you. He won't speak on his own, but only what he hears from the Father, and he will reveal prophetically to you what is to come. He will glorify me on the earth, for he will receive from me what is mine and reveal it to you. Everything that belongs to the Father belongs to me—that's why I say that the Divine Encourager will receive what is mine and reveal it to you."
>
> — John 16:13–15, TPT

Are you feeling hopeful about your future? If not, or if you're unsure, do you think a touch of encouragement from the Lord would help? If your answer is yes, I have good news for you!

The Holy Spirit is living inside of you, if you have received Jesus Christ as your Savior. You have been presented with a glorious gift from God the Father—His Holy Spirit as your Divine Teacher and Encourager. This Wonderful Counselor will not only reveal insight into things ahead, He will help you to pray into the blessed future He has designed for you (Jeremiah 29:11).

Savor these precious promises from Romans 8:26–28 (TPT):

> *"And in a similar way, the Holy Spirit takes hold of us in our human frailty to empower us in our weakness. For example, at times we don't even know how to pray, or know the best things to ask for. But the Holy Spirit rises up within us to super-intercede on our behalf, pleading to God with emotional sighs too deep for words. God, the searcher of the heart, knows fully our longings, yet he also understands the desires of the Spirit, because the Holy Spirit passionately pleads before God for us, his holy ones, in perfect harmony with God's plan and our destiny. So we are convinced that every detail of our lives is continually woven together for good, for we are his lovers who have been called to fulfill his designed purpose."*

The Holy Spirit can impart hope, offer timely direction of the supernatural kind, and share eternal truths that transcend our temporal state or experience. Nothing compares to hearing from your Creator.

At times, particularly for new believers, or when persevering through a dry or difficult season, a bit of guidance can be helpful in tuning our spiritual ears to hear Him speak.

Devotional books are an abundant resource to aid in this regard. They shine a light on Scripture by revealing insights the author gained through his or her own study, experience, or in prayer. By nature, devotionals can be a wonderful tool to help the reader draw near to the Lord and receive revelation into His Word. Some months before my caregiving season began, I received a uniquely delivered lesson about living in the power of God's strength, and not relying on my own—a principle that would prove essential for the years ahead.

My journal notes from that day speak of a dream from which I had just awakened, shortly before I would read a strikingly similar devotional passage:

> *Thursday a.m.—very early, dreamt about being out in various (vacation?) settings...trees, people, buildings. Then I and a couple (standing nearby) saw a city in the distance. I asked about power for the city, and (the lady) pointed to a huge waterfall—I could see the water falling over turbines to make energy.*

This was a somewhat unusual dream for me, on an unfamiliar subject, and quite specific in detail. Imagine my amazement when I picked up my devotional booklet, opened it to that day's entry, and began reading about Niagara Falls![1] The author explained that the flow of water from the river leading to this massive waterfall is diverted through turbines to generate power for nearby areas—precisely what I had just visualized in my dream! He went on to discuss the power of meekness under God's control.

Clearly, had I not dreamed of a waterfall and turbines that morning, the devotional reading would not have had near the impact, such that years later I am still considering the significance of its preparatory message for my caregiving season. It became for me a beautiful example of how the Holy Spirit can highlight biblical concepts through dreams and other means of inspiration to provide needed revelation for our journey through life. You are never alone! You have been gifted with a Divine Teacher and Encourager who lives in you. The Holy Spirit is interceding for you and will lead you into all truth. Invite Him to guide you, and wait upon Him in faith and expectancy.

Reflection and Application

Think about the times you've heard clearly from the Lord. In what manner did He speak? Can you find examples in Scripture of the Lord delivering messages in a similar way? Ask the Holy Spirit to reveal truths from His Word in new and unique ways—in such a way that you know without a doubt that you've heard from Him. If you feel Him speaking to you through Scripture, take note as soon as possible after you've received insight to best capture the full revelation.

Quickly make note of your dreams after waking to ensure the details aren't forgotten. Consider investing in one of the many Christian books on dream interpretation.

Prayer of Declaration

> *Heavenly Father, thank You for Your Holy Spirit, my Divine Teacher and Encourager! I'm so grateful to know He intercedes for me and for His revelation of truth. Help me to accurately interpret every form of divine inspiration I receive. With the Holy Spirit's help, I will fulfill every purpose You have for my life. In the name of Jesus, I pray. Amen.*

Day 5—With Him, All Things Are Possible

"But Jesus looked at them and said to them, 'With men this is impossible, but with God all things are possible.'"

— Matthew 19:26, NKJV

Have you ever believed for the impossible—and watched it become *possible*?

I have! My faith for a seeming impossibility became sight, and what a beautiful feeling it was.

During my first year at a new church, I became aware of a significant debt owed on the mortgage. Upon hearing the large figure, I recall a strong sense of something rising up in my inner being, which I recognized as an impartation of faith to believe for that mountain of debt to be moved! I had no idea when or how it would come to pass…I just knew beyond any doubt that I was to believe for it.

I began to pray and to speak declarations over our church for debt freedom. Some days, I would drive by the church, roll down my window, and shout, "Thank You, God, for a debt-free church!" Going into the church before a service, I'd pause outside the front door, place my hand on the building and declare it debt-free, giving praise to God for the miracle —as if it had already occurred.

You can imagine my excitement when, after a period of months, it was announced, "The church is paid off!" For me, and I believe for everyone who had been praying in faith, that declaration was like heavenly music—a sweet sound, indeed!

Oh, that the answers would always come so quickly and in line with our expectations. Though, in each situation, we can always anchor our trust in the unwavering goodness of God regardless of circumstances as they may appear.

Have you ever believed for something seemingly impossible, but it *didn't* turn out as you had hoped?

I, too, have shared that experience.

For believers, it can be difficult to understand why, for example, some are healed in answer to prayer while others are not. Though we take comfort in the assurance that our loved ones, who have received salvation through faith in Christ, will enjoy divine health at their transition to Heaven, our desire is to see healing come forth in this realm. We know that Jesus fully paid for our healing by His stripes,[1] so we wonder why it doesn't always manifest fully in the natural.

During her latter years, I prayed in faith for Mother's healing from dementia and cancer. As time went on with no evidence of that coming to pass, I fought waves of unbelief, and at times felt as though my faith for her miracle was wavering, though I knew Jesus had already made provision for it.

I may never know, this side of Heaven, what my prayers for Mother accomplished. But I have entrusted it all to God, knowing He is good. Like the old hymn,[2] my soul can sing "it is well" and remain at peace, assured that the pursuits of my faith are secure in His loving care.

One thing I do know—despite the afflictions of late stage dementia that attacked her body, Mother never lost her awareness of who I was. Even visitors to our home would remark about how Mother still knew me and how her face would light up when I walked into the room, even in the days leading to her homegoing.

In her final weeks here, with much of her ability to communicate stolen by disease, Mother was still able to express her appreciation to me for keeping her at home. Such comfort and joy that brought to my heart, at the end of a long and arduous season of caregiving, as I was having to release my beloved mother from this life into eternity.

I suppose you could say it was a departing gift of love from a mother to her daughter.

A seeming impossibility, given the natural circumstances? Perhaps a heavenly answer to a daughter's prayer in faith.

REFLECTION AND APPLICATION

What impossibility in your life is poised to be overturned by Almighty God working through your faith-filled belief?

Is anything hindering you from standing in faith over that situation? Seek inspiration from the Holy Spirit and Scripture to help you exercise the faith God has given you, and believe beyond what you see with your natural eyes to what He can accomplish supernaturally.

PRAYER OF DECLARATION

> *Heavenly Father, I know that Your Word is eternally true, and that with You, nothing shall be impossible! I gratefully receive the measure of faith that You have promised, and I rest in the sufficiency of Your precious gift. Transform my faith to sight, to see impossibilities become possibilities, as I cooperate with Your Holy Spirit. In the name of Jesus, I pray. Amen.*

Day 6—Perfectly Peaceful

"Rejoice in the Lord always. Again I will say, rejoice! Let your gentleness be known to all men. The Lord is at hand. Be anxious for nothing, but in everything by prayer and supplication, with thanksgiving, let your requests be made known to God; and the peace of God, which surpasses all understanding, will guard your hearts and minds through Christ Jesus."

— Philippians 4:4–7, NKJV

Have you ever yearned for days filled with perfect peace? Do you wonder if that's even possible in this life with its demands and complexities, particularly with the addition of caregiving responsibilities?

God's Word offers wisdom from above to lead you there! In Philippians 4, the apostle Paul counsels believers to rejoice, pray, and give thanks—with the promised result of receiving God's peace.

Interestingly, in his letter to the church at Thessalonica, Paul identifies essentially the same actions as being God's will for the believer: *"Rejoice always, pray without ceasing, in everything give thanks; for this is the will of God in Christ Jesus for you"* (1 Thessalonians 5:16–18, NKJV).

May that scriptural promise be a great encouragement to you. Rest assured that, as you live in God's will—rejoicing always, praying continually, and giving thanks in every circumstance—you will receive His supernatural peace to guard your heart and mind. That's a prescription that won't cost you anything except obedience to His Word. Best of all, God's remedies come with guaranteed potency and no negative side effects!

As a caregiver, I diligently pursued peace in every aspect of my life. I knew it was essential to my ability to continue to keep Mother at home, as well as to my own well-being. Still, it seemed that situations beyond my control were constantly at war with the peace I was trying so desperately to maintain.

I knew that God's Word would not return to Him void but would accomplish the purpose for which He sent it forth (Isaiah 55:11). So, if His Word said I could expect perfect peace, and that my heart and mind would have His covering of protection, I was determined to take hold of that promise and not let go!

It came at one of my lowest points…that divine touch from the Master, imparting a peace that eclipsed every upsetting circumstance I faced.

Year after year had passed of my wondering if things would one day get better, easier, and if I would ever receive a true respite. Just when it seemed I would be overwhelmed by the perpetual deluge of obligations beyond my abilities, the Lord's comfort and strength came flooding in, enveloping me like a warm, gentle wave. It wasn't a physical sensation, and I couldn't see it with my eyes, but something was imparted to me, tangible enough to take hold of.

"JESUS! WHERE ARE YOU?!" was my cry of desperation from the bathroom floor as, once again, I had been constrained to attend to a mess there. Feeling utterly weary and totally abandoned to the drudgery of following an apparently endless trail of messes, I paused for a moment, hands and knees firmly planted on the tile floor.

As quickly as I had called upon His name, I sensed my will release to Him in surrender. It was as if something came over me that broke the power of the circumstances permeating my mother's bathroom that day. The anguish I had felt, though not removed, was suddenly overshadowed with quiet praise.

From the depths of my soul, the words came: "Thank You, Lord, for the *privilege* of caring for my mother," I said peacefully. "Thank You for the beautiful and terrible privilege—*because it's both*."

I had received a soothing measure of calming strength in my distress. My duties remained, and I was determined to carry on—however many days or years left in my service—in spite of the unpleasantries.

I wanted to please God in the doing. I knew that would involve offering praise instead of complaint, no matter the difficulty or discomfort of the task at hand. Still, the emotions of that day were very real, but not so much as the compelling desire of my loving Heavenly Father to comfort His child with supernatural peace in the midst of her suffering.

REFLECTION AND APPLICATION

What, if any, circumstances are hindering your ability to maintain perfect peace in every situation? Apply the scriptural guidelines given in Philippians 4 and 1 Thessalonians 5, and stand in faith and expectancy. Take note of and celebrate each victory and answer to prayer!

PRAYER OF DECLARATION

> *Heavenly Father, I am so grateful for the guidance*
> *You've given in Your Word on living in perfect peace*
> *and Your supernatural provision of comfort. May my*
> *rejoicing, prayers, and thanksgiving be pleasing*
> *to You, as I receive Your promised peace.*
> *In the name of Jesus, I pray. Amen.*

Part Two

Serving

"Every believer has received grace gifts, so use them to serve one another as faithful stewards of the many-colored tapestry of God's grace."

— 1 Peter 4:10, TPT

Day 7—Becoming a Servant

"The greatest among you will be the one who always serves others from the heart."

— Matthew 23:11, TPT

"You have your own life to live," they would gently say…my well-meaning friends…respectful of my desire to care for Mother yet observant of the cost. Caring advice, offered out of a heartfelt concern for me, which touched my heart.

To be honest, the thought had already occurred to me on more than one occasion.

It sounded good, on the surface. After all, I had plans for my life—good intentions to do important things that didn't include the mundane duties I found myself tending to day after day for years as a full-time caregiver. It's just that, despite my circumstances, I couldn't shake the reality of God's Word and its emphasis on serving.

> "Every Scripture has been inspired by the Holy Spirit, the breath of God. It will empower you by its instruction and correction, giving you the strength to take the right direction and lead you deeper into the path of godliness. Then you will be <u>God's servant</u>, fully mature and perfectly prepared to fulfill any assignment God gives you."
>
> — 2 Timothy 3:16–17, TPT (emphasis added)

I knew that, though my heart desired to plan my way, it was the Lord who would direct my steps (Proverbs 16:9), as long as I was walking in obedience to Him. This would involve placing the needs of others ahead of my own desires, becoming a servant and being faithful to the call until my service was complete.

It would also compel me to immerse myself in the Scriptures for answers to difficult questions, knowing the Holy Spirit would guide me. His Word is a lamp to our feet and a light to our path (Proverbs 119:105).

Though I never planned to be a stay-at-home daughter, I loved my mother dearly and wanted her to always have the best care. Not being the "nurse type," as Mother had affectionately informed me in my younger days, I had essentially resolved that caregiving was not in my future. If the day were to come in which she needed help with personal care, I reasoned, we could find a nice senior home for her—a place where others (the trained people) could attend to those needs. I, of course, would be a regular visitor and oversee her care.

That, however, was not Mother's plan. As a caregiver, who had experienced first-hand the benefits of keeping a loved one at home, she desired to live out her elder years with me. Given my career focus and busy life, that scenario wasn't easily fitting into my paradigm. But it was about to.

After years of resisting the idea, when the need presented itself, I realized the Lord had prepared me for the journey of servanthood to care for my mother. Nearing the end of that path, I would indeed be required to muster the strength and fortitude to override my somewhat sensitive nature toward all those unpleasant tasks I had diligently hoped to avoid. Gratefully, the Lord always met my need with His provision of supernatural perseverance for the long and arduous days (and nights), along with divine refreshment and dedicated helpers to come alongside when the task became too great for me alone.

As the One who came to serve and to give His life for many, Jesus was my Role Model for that season of bountiful blessings enveloped in extreme trials. Much like with a wrapped present, in which the initial focus is on the outer covering that must be removed to reveal the true gift, the trials of caregiving were very real and challenging, necessitating my utter reliance upon the Lord to endure. But the trials proved fleeting, and the time came to tear off and discard them like gift wrap, leaving only the gift given by the Giver.

My gift—to cherish for time and eternity—was my Giver's loving and strengthening Presence to sustain me throughout my time of greatest need, enabling me to provide for Mother during hers, and bringing me out with a testimony to share. Had it not been for the Gift-Giver's providential guidance and provision, I most surely would have opted out of the most meaningful and consequential season of my life...the one in which I became a servant.

Reflection and Application

Think about your own perceptions of servanthood. What priority do you place on serving others? Are there any relationships, whether for a loved one in your care or otherwise, in which you sense the Lord calling you deeper into service? Consider taking one step of faith into His prompting. If it involves a major life change, such as bringing a loved one home to live with you or meeting a need for enhanced care—seek counsel from a trusted leader, such as a pastor, and try to take it one step at a time. Be gentle and graceful with yourself and those involved, trusting the Lord to lead you forward.

Prayer of Declaration

Heavenly Father, thank You for promising to direct my steps. When those steps lead me on a journey of servanthood where my own desires must be set aside for the benefit of another, help me to serve joyfully from my heart. In the name of Jesus, I pray. Amen.

Day 8—His Command to Love

"So this is my command: Love each other deeply, as much as I have loved you. For the greatest love of all is a love that sacrifices all. And this great love is demonstrated when a person sacrifices his life for his friends."[1]

— John 15:12–13, TPT

How do we love in devoted obedience to the command of Jesus? One decision at a time.

Most of us may never be asked to literally sacrifice our lives to benefit another. We will, however, most surely experience decisions between tending to our own needs or desires, or focusing on another's well-being. These are opportune moments in which we can demonstrate our love through sacrifice.

One such occasion presented itself when I perceived the approaching time to prematurely end my 30-year career to stay home with Mother. It was not easy to transition from a significant part of my life that had been so satisfying and rewarding, but I knew it was in Mother's best interest. My decision was further hastened by my own acknowledgment that I couldn't do it all. Her needs and my own human limitations were becoming such that I was increasingly challenged to give my best at home and at work.

Adding to the equation, I had also recently begun serving as a volunteer with an orphan advocacy ministry that felt like a new calling for me, though I soon realized that I would have to release that as well.

Mother and I had reached a sort of tipping point. Our roles were reversing, and I was now in charge.

I didn't want to be in charge.

I wanted her to be normal again—my *mother*. But we had entered a stage where she was more like the daughter, and I, the mother. She was desiring (and needing) more time with me, and that growing attachment was a major factor in my decision to embrace the role of full-time caregiver.

One day, as I was getting ready for work—as she had observed many times before—Mother asked, "Are you going somewhere?" I replied, matter-of-factly, "Yes, I'm going to work," and continued with my preparations to head out the door. A few seconds later, she chuckled at herself and said, "I just started to cry!" I paused to give her a hug and tried to comfort her, saying, "It's nice to be wanted," and she added, "Or needed."

I understood her feelings. As a little girl, I was very attached to her. To this day, I'm deeply appreciative that she chose to be a stay-at-home mother. So, when she needed the extra help, it seemed appropriate for me to become a stay-at-home daughter to care for her.

From my journal: "Mother wasn't happy about my going to work and (the caregiver) coming. As I drove away, it appeared she was about to cry as she looked out her bedroom window. She said something like 'Hurry home!' Later, as I drove back into the driveway, she was standing at her window, clapping and waving!"

For about the next eight years, I was with her or close by. This was comforting to her, and it was a blessing for me not to have a career to maintain on top of all of my care management responsibilities.

Though there have been times I missed my career days, I've never regretted the choice to leave them behind to spend more time with Mother. The Lord was faithful, and our needs were always provided for. My caregiving season now past, I am left with gratitude and joy in the choice to forego other pursuits to focus on Mother. It was a beautiful opportunity given to me to offer to my dear one the blessing of sacrificial love.

Reflection and Application

In your everyday life, what does loving others in a sacrificial way look like? Are there any opportunities waiting for you, in which you could choose to sacrifice your preferences or needs to enhance the life of another? If so, consider one or two steps you can take to initiate that action and proceed forward, with God's help.

Prayer of Declaration

Heavenly Father, may my obedience to Your commands testify of my devotion to You, as I daily seek to love You with all that I am and to love my neighbor as myself. Open my eyes to see the opportunities You offer in which I can choose sacrificial love. In the name of Jesus, I pray. Amen.

Day 9—Giving Honor

"Be devoted to tenderly loving your fellow believers as members of one family. Try to outdo yourselves in respect and honor of one another."

— Romans 12:10, TPT

As I write this, we in the United States are observing Memorial Day, in which we honor those who have given the ultimate sacrifice in service to our country. Coming from a military family, the importance of honoring the men and women who served was instilled in me by my parents at an early age. For that, I am truly grateful.

I'm also very appreciative of wise teachers through the years who guided me along the scriptural path of honoring my parents—some knowingly, and others simply by their example.

> *"For the commandment, 'Honor your father and your mother,' was the first of the Ten Commandments with a promise attached: 'You will prosper and live a long, full life if you honor your parents.'"*
>
> — Ephesians 6:2–3, TPT

Now that Mother and Dad are both with the Lord, I can recall instances in which I wish I had taken more care to show them honor, and thankfully, times when I honored them in the way they deserved. In raising me, they willingly sacrificed to provide for my needs, and I owe them a debt of gratitude and honor.

Honor is due those who sacrifice for the benefit of another. Abandoning or postponing something we desire doesn't tend to come naturally, but when we are guided by love—seeking to honor another above ourselves—it affords greater meaning to our sacrificial service. Love motivates sacrifice, and when we choose to honor a loved one sacrificially, we clearly demonstrate the value we ascribe to them.

As caregivers, we may be called upon to sacrifice precious commodities, such as our time, career, finances, relationships, physical and emotional energy, and dreams for our own lives. But we receive honor as we willingly release these possessions to help (honor in action) our loved one. Honor blesses the one to whom it is directed *as well as* the giver.

As Mother's caregiver, some of my fondest memories are of the times I honored her well, and my biggest regrets are those instances when I lost my patience and did not treat her with the honor and respect she deserved. However, if we were able to ask her now, I believe Mother would say that she felt honored by the care I gave—even on the occasions when I, because of fatigue or irritation, offered less than I should have. Always so gracious and forgiving, she imparted the assurance that she understood my desire to honor her, regardless of how accurately my words or actions of the moment reflected that truth.

God's Word reveals rich insight into the concept of honor:

- Jesus honors the Father, and the Father honors Jesus (John 8:49, 54).
- God honors *us* when we set our love upon Him and when we serve Jesus (Psalm 91:14–15 and John 12:26).
- God's name is to be honored through singing (Psalm 66:2).
- Honoring the Lord with our possessions comes with a reward (Proverbs 3:9–10).
- Honoring our parents comes with a promise (Ephesians 6:2–3).
- We are to honor all people, including those in positions of leadership (1 Peter 2:17).
- Humility precedes honor (Proverbs 15:33).
- A humble spirit retains honor (Proverbs 29:23).

Honor can be likened to an investment. When we honor the Lord, we faithfully devote (invest) time in prayer and fellowship with Him, and we cheerfully manage the resources He has provided according to the guidance in His Word. When we honor others, we receive the blessing that honor brings by ascribing value (investing) into their lives.

In both cases, the returns are supernatural!

Reflection and Application

Read through the Scriptures on honor, and give thought to what it means to you. Identify a few ways that you are currently showing honor to others.

As the attribute that precedes honor, do a word study on humility (see also humble), and personalize it with practical steps of obedience to the Scriptures. To help you get started, here are a few verses:

- *"By humility and the fear of the Lord, are riches and honor and life"* (Proverbs 22:4, NKJV).
- *"Therefore, as the elect of God, holy and beloved, put on tender mercies, kindness, humility, meekness, longsuffering; bearing with one another, and forgiving one another, if anyone has a complaint against another; even as Christ forgave you, so you also must do. But above all these things put on love, which is the bond of perfection"* (Colossians 3:12–14, NKJV).
- *"Likewise you younger people, submit yourselves to your elders. Yes, all of you be submissive to one another, and be clothed with humility, for 'God resists the proud, But gives grace to the humble.' Therefore humble yourselves under the mighty hand of God, that He may exalt you in due time, casting all your care upon Him, for He cares for you"* (1 Peter 5:5–7, NKJV).

(Treat yourself to a bonus by also studying the fear of the Lord.)

Prayer of Declaration

> *Heavenly Father, increase my comprehension of the concept of honor, and teach me how I can more fully offer it to You and others. I dedicate myself to giving honor and conducting my actions in humility. Help me to be aware when I fall short of Your best in this regard, as I desire to please You in all things. In the name of Jesus, I pray. Amen.*

Day 10—Perseverance for the Journey

"And let us not grow weary while doing good, for in due season we shall reap if we do not lose heart."

— Galatians 6:9, NKJV

Do an internet search on what caregivers need most, and you'll find an abundance of good advice on topics such as respite, help with caregiving tasks and management, and resources for physical, emotional, and financial support.

One necessity, however, that doesn't frequently appear on "Most Needed" lists is the quality of perseverance.

Caregivers need perseverance for their journey—both for *time*, to maintain their ability to give care for the duration, and for *intensity*, to handle increasingly difficult situations without being overcome by weariness and fatigue.

As Galatians 6:9 indicates, it is possible to grow weary and lose heart while we are doing good—with a resulting loss of our harvest! That wouldn't be anyone's plan when assuming caregiving duties. Rather, the desire is to do good and be a blessing, achieving success in helping another person and persevering as long as they have a need.

Perseverance doesn't come easily or automatically, but it does bring rewards.

When you're running a race, armed with details such as the distance you'll have to run and whether the track is flat or hilly, straight or curvy, you can plan ahead and pace yourself for your best performance. With caregiving, there are so many variables and unknowns that trying to pace yourself can be quite a challenge. And if a caregiving season continues for a long period of time, it becomes much harder to surge (physically, emotionally, or even financially) to handle an increasing intensity of care needs.

Factor in the inability to plan for duration in many cases, as the one you are caring for may experience waves of illness intermixed with periods of improved health.

For me, this was one of the more arduous emotional aspects of caring for Mother, as she would occasionally share her sense of the approaching time of her homegoing (not in a fearful way, but in an awareness that the time was near). I would try to prepare myself based on her cues, and then her condition and strength would improve…which, of course, was a good thing. It was the swings back and forth that were challenging to handle, as this pattern began in earnest several years before she actually passed. During this time, I had to keep reminding myself to trust in the Lord and not rely on my own understanding, knowing that He was directing our paths (Proverbs 3:5–6).

As the duration of my caregiving season continued on and my tasks became more physically exhausting, I began to wonder if it were even possible for me to persist through to the end. My desire to protect and care for Mother had not diminished, but at a certain point, her needs superseded my abilities—even with professional caregiver assistance.

Yet in the most difficult of times, when I felt my own strength and patience waning, the idea of putting her in a care facility was still incomprehensible to me. I knew I would have to rely on supernatural strength from the Lord and the assistance of a small army of caregivers and other helpers.

I am so grateful the Lord enabled me to persevere and provided the help, helpers, and resources needed for Mother's care at home. All the while, I was gaining the reward of character and hope, according to Romans 5:3–5 (TPT): *"Even in times of trouble we have a joyful confidence, knowing that our pressures will develop in us patient endurance. And patient endurance will refine our character, and proven character leads us back to hope. And this hope is not a disappointing fantasy, because we can now experience the endless love of God cascading into our hearts through the Holy Spirit who lives in us!"*

What a reward it is!

REFLECTION AND APPLICATION

Read Romans 5:3–5 in a few different translations of the Bible. Try to identify a period of tribulation you previously endured in which the Lord developed your perseverance, character, and hope. Make note of your spiritual growth as you progressed through that adversity—it will be an encouragement to you and a resource to apply when you face future challenges requiring perseverance.

Jesus said we would have tribulations in this world, but that we should be of good cheer because He has overcome the world (John 16:33). Are you currently persevering through any tribulations, troubles, or sorrows? Apply Romans 5:3–5 and John 16:33, along with any other Scriptures that are meaningful to you, and write a personal prayer of declaration according to these verses.

Prayer of Declaration

> *Heavenly Father, I thank You that Jesus has overcome the world. I declare that I will live my life in good cheer in accordance with Your Word and with gratefulness for all Jesus has accomplished for me. With Your help, I will not grow weary in doing good and will reap the harvest You have for me! In times when I'm persevering through troubles or sorrows, I will be encouraged, knowing that You are with me—and, as my Redeemer, You will work all things together for good.*
> *In the name of Jesus, I pray. Amen.*

Day 11—As Unto Him

"Put your heart and soul into every activity you do, as though you are doing it for the Lord himself and not merely for others."

— Colossians 3:23, TPT

Caregiver, if you've had thoughts that your life doesn't have much meaning, *think again* in the context of today's Scripture. Imagine it—Almighty God has bestowed upon you the honor of serving the King of kings through serving your loved one. A high calling with high privilege, and with promised rich rewards.

"Then the King will turn to those on his right and say, 'You have a special place in my Father's heart. Come and experience the full inheritance of the kingdom realm that has been destined for you from before the foundation of the world! For when you saw me hungry, you fed me. When you found me thirsty, you gave me drink. When I had no place to stay, you invited me in, and when I was poorly clothed, you covered me. When I was sick, you tenderly

cared for me, and when I was in prison you visited me.' Then the godly will answer him, 'Lord, when did we see you hungry or thirsty and give you food and something to drink? When did we see you with no place to stay and invite you in? When did we see you poorly clothed and cover you? When did we see you sick and tenderly care for you, or in prison and visit you?' And the King will answer them, 'Don't you know? When you cared for one of the least of these, my little ones, my true brothers and sisters, you demonstrated love for me.'"

— Matthew 25:34–40, TPT

Jesus has placed a divine emphasis on serving. As we see in Mark 10:45, He affirms servanthood as a primary purpose for His coming.

If we are to serve others as unto the Lord, no reason remains to view caregiving as inferior to any other endeavor. The enemy of our souls may try to convince otherwise by offering an emotional trap of resentment against God and our loved one. We must take his lies captive and contend to bring our every thought into obedience to Christ (2 Corinthians 10:5).

Many times during my caregiving years, I had to actively resist the temptation to give in to feelings of resentment… It was one of the greatest battles I faced, especially when it seemed my own desires and dreams were continually being put on hold year after year in deference to responsibilities at home.

One such example was not being free to come and go as I pleased, particularly on Sundays when I would have preferred to gather with my church family and participate in our worship service.

Of course, it is beneficial to join and serve in a local congregation. The Bible encourages us not to forsake gathering together (Hebrews 10:24–25). However, caring for a loved one at home can, at times, present unique challenges to attending church or other events. While I was so grateful for online options that enabled me to maintain connection with this important part of my life, still there were times that I voiced frustration with having to miss in-person services.

As was so often the case, my perceptive mother helped me to gain a new perspective on the issue.

One Sunday, while busily attending to our morning routine and watching the time fly, my chances of making it to church were getting slimmer and slimmer. I said something to Mother (probably in my best disappointed tone of voice) about not being sure if I'd make it to church that day. My thoughts were likely more aligned with, "Well, I'm stuck here again, and I can't even get to *church*!"

Mother replied sweetly, "When you stay with me, that's the best thing you can do!" Holding up her oatmeal cookie with peanut butter, she continued, "I can't get it myself."

Oh, my! That statement of truth should have silenced any future complaining from me. But there was another time when I was fighting frustration at having to miss church. With great insight into the value of serving, Mother instructed, "When you're with me, you *are* at church!"

In her childlike reflection of Christlike love, my mother may have just as well quoted James 1:27 (TPT): *"True spirituali-*

ty that is pure in the eyes of our Father God is to make a difference in the lives of the orphans, and widows in their troubles, and to refuse to be corrupted by the world's values."

What higher calling could there be than to minister to Jesus by embracing true spirituality in devoting our life to serve another?

Reflection and Application

Think about your attitude toward serving and how well you've been putting Colossians 3:23 into practice. Set your sights this week on purposefully carrying out your caregiving tasks with an intentional focus on serving Jesus as you serve your loved one. At week's end, evaluate the results!

Prayer of Declaration

Heavenly Father, thank You for the privilege of serving my loved one, and for the honor of simultaneously serving Jesus. Strengthen me when I feel weary, and help me to take disappointing or resentful thoughts captive immediately so I will not come into agreement—even for one moment—with the lies of the enemy. May my attitude in my service honor my loved one, and may it glorify You and always bring You pleasure. In the name of Jesus, I pray. Amen.

Part Three

Believing

"Jesus said to him, 'If you can believe, all things are possible to him who believes.'"

— Mark 9:23, NKJV

Day 12—Faith That Pleases God

"But without faith it is impossible to please Him, for he who comes to God must believe that He is, and that He is a rewarder of those who diligently seek Him."

— Hebrews 11:6, NKJV

I've heard it said that fear and faith operate similarly. When we exercise our faith, we believe for something unseen, whether it is based on God's Word, a promise, or a prayer. Likewise, when we fear something, we activate faith for that very fear to materialize. We read in Job 3:25: *"For the thing I greatly feared has come upon me, and what I dreaded has happened to me."* Job evidently had active fear working in his thoughts (equating to and operating like faith) for what he dreaded.

How often caregivers are confronted with some scenario to dread! Prognosticators from every direction present fearsome predictions for your future and that of your loved one…"Well, you know dementia *always gets worse*," or "Caregiving will take a *toll* on you," or "You're going to go *broke* paying for all this!"

Dear caregiver, resist the temptation to succumb to worry and dread. Choose to break the power of fear and *empower your faith!* With courage and determination, take hold of His Word in your mind and heart. Remember, what you are seeing in the natural may be factual, but facts are subject to change. God's Word is living and powerful (Hebrews 4:12). It will never return to Him void (Isaiah 55:11) and will by no means pass away (Matthew 24:35).

Take your stand on God's promises and boldly declare His eternally truthful Word over your situation:

- "My loved one is healed by the stripes of Christ, and has been given a sound mind by Almighty God!" (1 Peter 2:5, 2 Timothy 1:7).
- "I will not receive a toll from the enemy—Jesus has defeated him. I am a victor in Christ, and He always causes me to triumph!" (Colossians 2:15, 2 Corinthians 2:14).
- "I'm not going broke—my God shall supply all my need. He is my Shepherd, and I shall not want!" (Philippians 4:19, Psalm 23:1).

If we know that it is impossible to please God without faith, clearly there is an imperative on seeking it. As always, the recipe and roadmap are found within His Word.

- *"Faith is the substance of things hoped for, the evidence of things not seen. By faith, the elders obtained a good*

testimony. *By faith, the worlds were framed by the Word of God, and things which are seen were not made of anything visible"* (Hebrews 11:1–3, NKJV).
- The righteous live by faith (Hebrews 10:38).
- Faith comes by hearing, and hearing by God's Word (Romans 10:17)—a good reason to read (and sing[1]) the Word aloud!
- Jesus said, *"Have faith in God. For assuredly, I say to you, whoever says to this mountain, 'Be removed and be cast into the sea,' and does not doubt in his heart, but believes that those things he says will be done, he will have whatever he says. Therefore I say to you, whatever things you ask when you pray, believe that you receive them, and you will have them"* (Mark 11:22–24, NKJV).

Jesus marveled at great faith and great lack of faith.

In this passage from Matthew 8, we find the Savior marveling at the faith of a centurion who understood authority:

"When Jesus had entered Capernaum, a centurion came to Him, pleading with Him, saying, "Lord, my servant is lying at home paralyzed, dreadfully tormented." And Jesus said to him, "I will come and heal him." The centurion answered and said, "Lord, I am not worthy that You should come under my roof. But only speak a word, and my servant will be healed. For I also am a man under authority, having soldiers under me. And I say to this one, 'Go,' and he goes; and to another, 'Come,' and he comes..." When Jesus heard it, He marveled, and said to those who followed, "Assuredly, I say to you, I have not found such great faith, not even in Israel! ...Then Jesus said to the centurion, "Go your way; and as you have

believed, so let it be done for you." And his servant was healed that same hour."

— MATTHEW 8:5–10, 13, NKJV

Determine today that you will exercise the full measure of faith God has given you to take hold of every blessing He has provided for you and your loved ones. My prayer for you as you contend is taken from Colossians 2:6 (TPT): *"In the same way you received Jesus our Lord and Messiah by faith, continue your journey of faith, progressing further into your union with him!"*

REFLECTION AND APPLICATION

Give thought to what it would take for you to develop faith strong enough to make Jesus marvel. Ask the Lord for guidance on how to get started as you meditate on Hebrews 11:6, and take the first step.

PRAYER OF DECLARATION

*Heavenly Father, it is my earnest desire to please You.
I know that You reward those who diligently seek You.
Today, I commit to diligence in seeking You
all the days of my life, that I may develop
a faith that causes You to marvel!
In the name of Jesus, I pray. Amen.*

Day 13—Your Words Declare

"You will also declare a thing, And it will be established for you."

— Job 22:28, NKJV

When I was a little girl, I unknowingly put this principle into practice. Now that I am older, the fruit of my declaration has endured.

Mother was helping me to understand how to properly converse with a new acquaintance. As I recall, this was in response to a conversation I'd just had with a neighbor lady who evidently fell into this category… Mother explained that some ladies were sensitive about their age, so it would be best *not* to ask how old they were. (You probably guessed it— I had asked.)

I recall a struggle to comprehend this at the time, as it made absolutely no sense to me. I loved my age! I had a birthday party each year to celebrate my age. How could anyone have a problem with their age?

Having reached my mid-sixties, I now understand the concept more clearly, though it is one that has never been an issue for me. At the tender age of eight or nine years old, I made a decree over my life—without even knowing what I was doing. After mulling over what Mother had just shared and not coming up with any better answers, I declared to her, "I'm going to like EVERY age!" And, since that day, I have.

To take it a step further, declaring God's Word is much more significant than simply making a positive statement. By speaking His Word, we can initiate the activation of His will. Jesus instructed His disciples to pray, *"Your will be done on earth as it is in heaven"* (Matthew 6:10, NKJV).

Patricia King explains it best in her book *The Power of the Decree: Releasing the Authority of God's Word Through Declaration*:

> "A decree is an official order issued by a legal governmental authority. It is different from either a confession or a proclamation in that it is brought forth through governmental initiation. In other words, a decree carries much more authority than does a confession or proclamation. In the Old Testament, one Hebrew word commonly used for decree is *kathab*, which is defined as a 'written edict of royal enactment, of divine authority.' (Strong's Concordance #3791) ... This makes a decree made in the name of Jesus our King even more powerful, because He is for all eternity the King of all kings (Revelation 19:16). There is no authority greater than that of Christ Jesus. And when you speak His Word, it carries incomparable weight and power —it will not be revoked!"[1]

Wow! Now there's a great motivator to seek and speak declarations from God's Word. His will is revealed in His Word that is backed by His authority. Declaring His Word is a powerful means to contend for His will to come forth in our lives and the lives of our loved ones.

Scriptures for declaration:

- Deuteronomy 28:1–14 is a beautiful passage reflecting the desires of the Father's heart to bestow abundant blessings upon His children who choose obedience.
- *"So you shall serve the Lord your God, and He will bless your bread and your water. And I will take sickness away from the midst of you. No one shall suffer miscarriage or be barren in your land; I will fulfill the number of your days"* (Exodus 23:25–26, NKJV).
- *"The Lord shall preserve you from all evil; He shall preserve your soul. The Lord shall preserve your going out and your coming in from this time forth, and even forevermore"* (Psalm 121:7–8, NKJV).
- The Lord is our Shield (Psalm 3:3).
- The Whole Armor of God (Ephesians 6:13–18).
- *"And my God shall supply all your need according to His riches in glory by Christ Jesus"* (Philippians 4:19, NKJV).
- Blessings on tithing (Malachi 3:10).
- Blessings on giving (Luke 6:38).
- We were, and are, healed by the stripes (wounds) of Christ (Isaiah 53:5 and 1 Peter 2:24).
- *"I will both lie down in peace, and sleep; For You alone, O Lord, make me dwell in safety"* (Psalm 4:8, NKJV).

Choose wisely the words you speak!

REFLECTION AND APPLICATION

Search the Scriptures for declarations. Make note of those that are particularly meaningful to you and begin to declare them (speak them aloud) regularly. To get started, read Psalm 16 and see how many individual verses can be spoken as a declaration of blessing. Remember that God's Word will not return to Him void (Isaiah 55:11), which is another declaration you can make over your decrees.

As you go through your week, pay attention to the words you speak. If you find that you are speaking something contrary to God's Word, renounce what you've said and replace it by declaring a scriptural truth over the situation.

PRAYER OF DECLARATION

Heavenly Father, when You spoke, creation came forth. You have made me in Your image. Help me to more fully understand the importance of speaking Your eternally truthful and powerful words to see Your will be done on earth as it is in Heaven. In the name of Jesus, I pray. Amen.

Day 14—Think on These Things

"Finally, brethren, whatever things are true, whatever things are noble, whatever things are just, whatever things are pure, whatever things are lovely, whatever things are of good report, if there is any virtue and if there is anything praiseworthy—meditate on these things."

— Philippians 4:8, NKJV

Think about what you think about (meditate on).

- Do you typically think true and noble, pure and lovely thoughts that align with God's Word, or do you more often find yourself focusing on the negative, including the lies of the enemy that are contrary to scriptural truth?
- When an adverse report on your health or finances suddenly interrupts your peaceful existence, do your immediate thoughts gravitate toward the truth of

God's Word and His report or the worst case scenario?
- How successful are you at pondering the praiseworthy and virtuous aspects of your daily activities and interactions with others, including those on social media?

What we focus our thoughts on has a direct impact upon how we live our lives. In Proverbs 23:7, we read that as a man thinks in his heart, so is he. Think on that sobering thought!

Knowing the importance of our thoughts—and our spoken words that flow from them—we can easily see why the Lord has placed such an emphasis on right thinking in His Word. Our adversary who comes only to steal, kill, and destroy may be prevented from carrying out his evil schemes against us. Though he works overtime to convince us of his threats, we can extinguish all of his fiery darts with our God-given Shield of Faith.

As Mother's only child and without any other family members close by, whenever I faced a health challenge, I found myself overly concerned about my ability to care for her for the long term. Of course, I wanted to be there for her; however, the fear of something happening to me that would prevent me from caring for her was revealing a lack of faith on my part. I knew I needed to submit that to the Lord, to entrust our circumstances into His capable hands, to keep my thoughts focused on His promises, and to live in a state of *trust* instead of *worry*. What a testimony He would provide, as I sought to do just that.

Day 14—Think on These Things 85

While Mother was still with me, I had a benign skin issue that needed attention, so I went to the dermatologist. The doctor explained that my options were to either do nothing and watch the area or undergo a simple surgical procedure that should take care of it, though I might need another procedure after that. She then said that though it was minor, there were always risks, listing out a series of possible negative outcomes. Her recommendation was to do the procedure, so I scheduled the appointment.

It was a cold, gray December morning when I got in the car to drive across town to her office. The 25-minute drive was uneventful on the outside, but my thoughts were churning on the inside. I was struggling with an irrational fear, though trying my best to trust in the Lord and keep my focus on His Word. I wasn't afraid of the procedure or even the undesirable outcomes, as the risks were minimal and the procedure was routine. Still, thoughts kept coming to me: *Was I doing the right thing by getting the procedure? What if this, and what if that?!* I desperately wanted to feel the peace of the Lord but was struggling to take hold of it.

As I exited the freeway to proceed to the doctor's office, I recall saying out loud, "*Lord! I just need to know You're WITH me!*" Of course, I knew He was, but I couldn't seem to cast off that gripping fear.

Then, perhaps a mile or so down the road, as I was approaching a church I had attended many years earlier, I was astounded by the sight! There, in the front lawn of the church, was a manger scene…a 20-foot tall wood frame outline of a barn-like structure, adorned only with a single wooden manger with hay, along with huge letters spelling out the Christmas message: "GOD WITH US." And, as I slowed down to take it all in, I exclaimed, "*Of course,* You're with me, Lord. It's Your *Name!* Immanuel—God With Us!"

As you can imagine, the turmoil I had been feeling immediately shifted from fear to faith—with a simple reminder of His name.

So, the next time you're struggling with tormenting thoughts about yourself or the dear one you're caring for…remember that you are a child of Almighty God, and He sent His only Son, Jesus, Immanuel, as a reminder that He is always with you. He loves you and your loved one with an everlasting love. If you belong to Jesus, He is your refuge and fortress (Psalm 91:2), and no one can snatch you from His hand (John 10:28). That thought, alone, should help you keep your thoughts on all things true, noble, pure, and lovely.

Reflection and Application

Can you recall a time in which the Lord comforted you or helped you bring negative thoughts into obedience to His Word? If you are struggling in this area, apply this powerful Scripture that will help you align your thoughts with His: *"We can demolish every deceptive <u>fantasy</u> that opposes God and break through every arrogant <u>attitude</u> that is raised up in defiance of the true knowledge of God. We capture, like prisoners of war, every <u>thought</u> and insist that it bow in obedience to the Anointed One"* (2 Corinthians 10:5, TPT, emphasis added).

Prayer of Declaration

Heavenly Father, thank You for helping me to bring my every thought into obedience to Christ. I desire to think and speak according to Your will and Word. In the name of Jesus, I pray. Amen.

Day 15—Stand, Therefore

"Stand therefore, having girded your waist with truth, having put on the breastplate of righteousness, and having shod your feet with the preparation of the gospel of peace; above all, taking the shield of faith with which you will be able to quench all the fiery darts of the wicked one. And take the helmet of salvation, and the sword of the Spirit, which is the word of God; praying always with all prayer and supplication in the Spirit ..."

— Ephesians 6:14–18, NKJV

The Lord has provided *His* armor for our protection. As we take it up and put it on, we are enabled to stand in His power. As a caregiver, each new day brought reminders of my utter reliance upon God's provision... I always knew it was there, but how sweet was the savor of success when faith became sight after standing on His Word!

I recall a time when I had to stand while feeling weak, believing for His provision of strength and for help when I had no promise of it—other than in His Word.

They (the caregiving experts) often emphasize: Don't try to do it all. Get help as needed and take respites frequently. Come to find out, they are right. In my experience as a family caregiver, this admonition falls squarely into the category of "easier said than done."

I had stayed home with Mother for eight years without leaving her overnight for a break. I didn't really think I needed one, but I got one anyway…at the hospital. One morning, as I was making breakfast, I started feeling a bit weary, and after talking with my doctor, I went in to have a few things checked out. Thankfully, all was well. I had just gotten a bit worn down.

It was nice for a couple of days to have meals brought to my room and not to have any responsibilities except to rest. But my short stay there abruptly ended with the forecast of an impending snowstorm. I needed to get back home, as I didn't have anyone to stay multiple nights (if need be) with Mother. But I wasn't sure I was feeling up to being Mother's sole caregiver for days on end, either. I left the hospital and began a search for someone to help.

Trying to arrange for a caregiver to come out that evening and possibly stay until the snow melted was another thing. I called some agencies, but most of their staff members were already scheduled with existing clients due to the incoming inclement weather. Finally, I found an agency willing to try to find a caregiver for us. The agency director and his registered nurse arrived at our home a couple of hours before the snow was to start. After evaluating our situation and making some calls, they found a caregiver willing to help.

As we continued to go through the required paperwork, they received a phone call—a bridge had just closed before the caregiver made it over, leaving no viable route for her to reach my home. The director looked at his RN, and she looked at him with tears in her eyes. "That's it… We don't have anyone else, do we?" she asked.

"No," he said.

Snow flurries in the darkening sky signaled the time for their departure, as they needed to get home before the road conditions deteriorated. They looked at me with great compassion, knowing they had to leave me alone, just out of the hospital, to care for Mother.

At that moment, I had to settle in my heart that God's grace and provision was sufficient.

"Do not worry about us," I told them, mustering as much faith as I could to decree: "The Lord will supply all our need. If I needed a caregiver here, I'd have one. Just pray for us. I'm trusting we'll be fine!" I was assured of God's blanket covering over Mother and me—no matter how many inches of snow were on the way.

The next morning, we were snowed in! Beholding the beauty of the sparkling white landscape outside my windows, I realized that, until the snow was cleared, we had no way out of my driveway and no one else could come in. As best I could, I pushed all concerns aside and began to praise the Lord and thank Him for the snow-removal team that He was sending.

Mind you, I had no idea how all of that snow would be cleared from our driveway. In our neighborhood, there had never been any snow removal services, but I believe in the power of decreeing God's Word, and I knew He would provide.

Around day three, I looked outside and *there they were!* My snow-removal team was coming down our street. A large pick-up truck with a plow was heading our way, followed by a mini earth-moving machine. Within a short time, our driveway and roads had been cleared for travel. As a bonus, the machinery ballet just outside our window captivated Mother and me!

Once again, the Lord had shown Himself faithful to His Word. When you've done all you know to do (according to His Word), stand—and keep standing!

Reflection and Application

Some people like to pray through Ephesians 6:10–18 and intentionally take up God's armor. Though His armor is spiritual, declaring His Word out loud and taking up the armor is helpful to activate our faith. Try it today…and stand.

Prayer of Declaration

> *Heavenly Father, thank You for providing Your armor for me. I stand victorious in Your armor! In the name of Jesus, I pray. Amen.*

Day 16—Choose Joy

> *"Join me, everyone! Let's praise the Lord together. Let's make him famous! Let's make his name glorious to all. Listen to my testimony: I cried to God in my distress and he answered me. He freed me from all my fears! Gaze upon him, join your life with his, and joy will come. Your faces will glisten with glory. You'll never wear that shame-face again."*
>
> — Psalm 34:3–5, TPT

As a caregiver, two primary things I depended upon from the Lord were joy and strength. I needed strength to manage my caregiving duties (and to persevere), and joy was the substance that fueled it. Though it was not always easy to choose joy, and there were plenty of times when I didn't necessarily feel joyful, I knew that the Lord's joy was my strength (Nehemiah 8:10), and so I pursued His joy with determination to take hold of the full measure!

I also understood that joy would be a healing balm for my tired body and weary emotions. Proverbs 17:22 (TPT) says, *"A joyful, cheerful heart brings healing to both body and soul. But the one whose heart is crushed struggles with sickness and depression."* If your heart today is feeling crushed, bring it before the Lord at His throne of grace (Hebrews 4:16). There, you will find mercy and grace to help in your time of need. He can give you a new heart (Ezekiel 36:26).

Joy is a quality of the fruit of the Spirit, and, as such, we can depend on the enablement of the Holy Spirit as we contend for it: *"But the fruit produced by the Holy Spirit within you is divine love in all its varied expressions: joy that overflows, peace that subdues, patience that endures, kindness in action, a life full of virtue, faith that prevails, gentleness of heart, and strength of spirit. Never set the law above these qualities, for they are meant to be limitless"* (Galatians 5:22–23, TPT).

To help us take hold of joy in the midst of challenges, here are a few key Scripture verses, including our lead Scripture for today. I encourage you to read these aloud or even sing them! You can make up your own melodies, and in doing so, sing a new song to the Lord (see first verse below):

- *"Compose new melodies that release new praises to the Lord. Play his praises on instruments with the anointing and skill he gives you. Sing and shout with passion; make a spectacular sound of joy—For God's Word is something to sing about"* (Psalm 33:3–4, TPT).
- *"You will show me the path of life; In Your presence is fullness of joy; At Your right hand are pleasures forevermore"* (Psalm 16:11, NKJV).

- "*My fellow believers, when it seems as though you are facing nothing but difficulties, see it as an invaluable opportunity to experience the greatest joy that you can! For you know that when your faith is tested it stirs up in you the power of endurance. And then as your endurance grows even stronger, it will release perfection into every part of your being until there is nothing missing and nothing lacking"* (James 1:2–4, TPT).
- *"… that you may walk worthy of the Lord, fully pleasing Him, being fruitful in every good work and increasing in the knowledge of God; strengthened with all might, according to His glorious power, for all patience and longsuffering with joy; giving thanks to the Father who has qualified us to be partakers of the inheritance of the saints in the light"* (Colossians 1:10–12, NKJV).
- *"Until now you've not been bold enough to ask the Father for a single thing in my name, but now you can ask, and keep on asking him! And you can be sure that you'll receive what you ask for, and your joy will have no limits"* (John 16:24, TPT).

As caregivers, we must remember that our countenance and disposition can influence our loved one (and others around us). In Philippians 4:4–7 (TPT), the apostle Paul offers helpful instruction on maintaining a joyful attitude, inside and out: *"Be cheerful with joyous celebration in every season of life. Let your joy overflow! And let gentleness be seen in every relationship, for our Lord is ever near. Don't be pulled in different directions or worried about a thing. Be saturated in prayer throughout each day, offering your faith-filled requests before God with overflowing gratitude. Tell him every detail of your life, then

God's wonderful peace that transcends human understanding, will guard your heart and mind through Jesus Christ."

So, today, may the Lord bless you with overflowing joy that will remain and bring healing to your body and soul. May joy spring up through you to refresh others and position you to receive His strength for your life's journey.

Reflection and Application

As you go about your activities this day, meditate on the supernatural joy of the Lord. As you do, thank Him for filling you with His joy that strengthens you. Consider singing your prayer to Him as a new song of praise!

Prayer of Declaration

Heavenly Father, thank You for so many promises in Your Word about joy! I desire to learn from You how to be joyful in every circumstance and to be a joy carrier so that others are drawn into Your supernatural joy. As I gaze upon You and join my life with Yours, thank You for making joy come to me, that I will experience fullness of joy in Your presence... and may my life and love bring You great joy. In the name of Jesus, I pray. Amen.

Part Four

Living

"... But I have come to give you everything in abundance, more than you expect—life in its fullness until you overflow!"

— John 10:10, TPT

Day 17—Your Story, Written in Heaven

"And in Your book they all were written, The days fashioned for me, When as yet there were none of them."

— Psalm 139:16, NKJV

Did you know that God ordained the days of your life before you were born, and they were inscribed in His book in Heaven? He created you with a free will, so you can choose your own steps or allow the Lord to direct them—but Your loving Heavenly Father thought of you and had plans for you long before your parents or even your grandparents (or great grandparents, and so on…) exchanged their first glance.

Regardless of the circumstances of your conception, or words that have been spoken over you by others, your life originated in God. He loves you dearly, and He holds you and the dear one you care for close in His thoughts.

Psalm 139 reveals beautiful truths of Father God's masterful creative plans and power as He meticulously designs and brings forth a human life. It is remarkable in its detailed insight imparted to King David. As you read through this Psalm, apply it in your thoughts to yourself and your loved one:

> *"You formed my innermost being, shaping my delicate inside and my intricate outside, and wove them all together in my mother's womb. I thank you, God, for making me so mysteriously complex! Everything you do is marvelously breathtaking. It simply amazes me to think about it! How thoroughly you know me, Lord! You even formed every bone in my body when you created me in the secret place; carefully, skillfully you shaped me from nothing to something. You saw who you created me to be before I became me! Before I'd ever seen the light of day, the number of days you planned for me were already recorded in your book. Every single moment you are thinking of me! How precious and wonderful to consider that you cherish me constantly in your every thought! O God, your desires toward me are more than the grains of sand on every shore!"*
>
> — Psalm 139:13–18, TPT

This wonderfully inspirational passage should awaken a desire in us to know God more intimately, to share that beautiful relationship with others, and to treasure His Word in our hearts (Psalm 119:11), that we may bring Him joy and fulfill every aspiration He has for our lives written in His book.

God's plans for us often exceed our own expectations, abilities, and even desires. When the Lord called Jeremiah to be a prophet, He said, *"Before I formed you in the womb I knew you;*

Before you were born I sanctified you; I ordained you a prophet to the nations" (Jeremiah 1:5, NKJV). This proclamation from God was met with apparent skepticism and perhaps a bit of trepidation in the young lad. He responded, *"'Ah, Lord God! Behold, I cannot speak, for I am a youth.' But the Lord said: 'Do not say, "I am a youth," For you shall go to all to whom I send you, And whatever I command you, you shall speak'"* (Jeremiah 1:6–7, NKJV).

Like me, you may feel totally unprepared and awkward with aspects of caregiving. And yet, you are making yourself available to the Lord, serving your loved one as unto Him. Your love, servant heart, and availability are all He needs to bring forth His divine purposes.

God is not looking for our abilities. He seeks our availability—and with that, we become like clay in the Hands of the Master Potter, ready to be transformed into a masterpiece and accomplish His purpose for our lives.

It is doubtful you'll find anyone who would say their life has gone according to God's best each day. At times, we make our own regrettable choices (Romans 7:15–25), yet as we humble ourselves and repent, God is faithful with swift mercy. And though we must also be aware of our adversary's intent to steal, kill, and destroy (John 10:10), Jesus came that we would have life more abundantly! He has equipped us to effectively stand against the enemy with weapons that are mighty through God to tear down strongholds (2 Corinthians 10:4). As we wield those weapons faithfully in the authority He has given us, we are empowered to extinguish every fiery dart of the enemy (read about the Whole Armor of God in Ephesians 6:10–18).

God is our Redeemer and can enable His plans to come forth in our lives as we submit to His will. Only He is able to take all of our bitter and sweet life experiences and cause them to work together for good, for those of us who love Him and are called according to His purposes (Romans 8:28).

Every soul is precious to God, our Creator and Heavenly Father. Let us honor Him with the life He has given us by yielding to His design and purposes. In doing so, we live out the pages of our story, written in Heaven.

Reflection and Application

Think about what your life would be like if you consistently lived each day perfectly aligned with God's will for you. Ask the Holy Spirit to reveal supernatural insight from the pages written about you in Heaven and for help to accomplish all that the Father has planned for you.

Prayer of Declaration

Heavenly Father, I submit my will to Yours and desire to live out the pages of my life in Your book—as You planned it long ago! Thank You for enabling and equipping me to do so, that my life will be pleasing to You and bring You glory. In the name of Jesus, I pray. Amen.

Day 18—Live in His Blessing

"Shout in celebration of praise to the Lord! Everyone who loves the Lord and delights in him will cherish his words and be blessed beyond expectation. Their descendants will be prosperous and influential. Every generation of the righteous will experience his favor."

— Psalm 112:1–2, TPT

Do you desire to live in the blessing and favor of the Lord?

What could be more comforting than to dwell every moment of every day in the assurance of our Heavenly Father's bountiful provision and protection? Oh, that we would awaken morning by morning secure in the knowledge of His ample supply and stroll through each day under a continuous sprinkling of blessing showers from Heaven. Perhaps you've tasted a bit of this blissful existence, as I have… How glorious it is!

But what should we do when unforeseen circumstances interrupt our contented state? God's Word guides us into all truth, leading the way to His blessing and favor through every situation.

Settle in your heart that the Word of God is not subject to change based on circumstances, whims, desires, or anything else that presents itself in opposition. As we read in Matthew 24:35 (NKJV): *"Heaven and earth will pass away, but My words will by no means pass away."* Building on that foundation, let's apply this scriptural guidance to our lives, and watch with anticipation for His favor and blessings to flow:

- *"Who may ascend into the hill of the Lord? Or who may stand in His holy place? He who has clean hands and a pure heart, Who has not lifted up his soul to an idol, Nor sworn deceitfully. He shall receive blessing from the Lord, And righteousness from the God of his salvation"* (Psalm 24:1–5, NKJV).
- *"He will bless those who fear the Lord, Both small and great"* (Psalm 115:13, NKJV).
- *"Great blessing and wealth fills the house of the wise, for their integrity endures forever. Even if darkness overtakes them, sunrise-brilliance will come bursting through because they are gracious to others, so tender and true"* (Psalm 112:3, TPT).
- *"Finally, all of you be of one mind, having compassion for one another; love as brothers, be tenderhearted, be courteous; not returning evil for evil or reviling for reviling, but on the contrary blessing, knowing that you were called to this, that you may inherit a blessing"* (1 Peter 3:8–9, NKJV).

While our circumstances may be subject to many factors, keeping our eyes on Him and resting in His Word will enable us to identify His blessings and favor, even in the most arduous situations.

When I became a caregiver, my life took on an entirely different form than I had planned…one for which I had very little context. Much like how a pilot flying in reduced visibility has to rely on instruments for safe navigation through a storm, I had to purposefully fix my attention on the Scriptures (and keep it there!) for guidance on how to successfully maneuver through the challenges I faced. My welfare and Mother's depended on it. Experienced pilots know that it would be to their peril to ignore the instruments while flying through reduced visibility. Because their natural instinct is to try to fly the plane by sight and feelings, they've had to undergo training to trust their instruments to help keep them on the prescribed flight path. In like manner, believers benefit from learning to rely on the tried and true guidance in Scripture for navigational help through the storms of life.

Looking back, I now see and can testify of His faithfulness that assured our safe journey through the turbulent times as well as on the clear days. Had I focused on the problems, instead of cherishing His Words, I would have never recognized the beautiful flow of His blessings and favor—right there in the midst of the challenges!

So, my word of encouragement for you today is this: Know that your Heavenly Father is a very good Father who loves to bless His children with good gifts. One of those gifts is His Word, filled with wisdom for navigating the sunny, easy paths of life, as well as those fraught with difficulty. As we follow His instructions, He is faithful to reward our obedience, and we will find ourselves living in His blessing, which overshadows any adversities that may come our way.

Reflection and Application

Count the ways you are living in the blessing of God or have received His favor. What areas in your life still need some attention in order for you to fully experience His blessing? Pray and ask the Holy Spirit for insight into how best to pursue it.

Prayer of Declaration

Heavenly Father, thank You for Your amazing generosity in making a way for me and my loved ones to live each day in Your blessing, even in the midst of difficulties. I dedicate myself to obedience to Your Word in order to invite Your uninterrupted blessings into my life. In faith, I gratefully and joyfully receive the abundance of Your favor and good gifts! Make me a carrier of Your blessing as I share Your goodness with others, and may I always be a blessing to You. In the name of Jesus, I pray. Amen.

Day 19—His Victory Is Yours

"But we thank God for giving us the victory as conquerors through our Lord Jesus, the Anointed One."

— 1 Corinthians 15:57, TPT

Battles are hard. No doubt about it. In this world, we know that we will encounter times of tribulation and spiritual warfare, but Jesus said we are to be of good cheer, for He has overcome the world (John 16:33). For the busy caregiver, in my experience, the most difficult times are those when the warfare seems continual with no cease fire.

Particularly during the latter part of my caregiving season, which over a period of years became increasingly more complex and challenging, it often felt as though I was facing concurrent spiritual battles while running on empty. It was hard, and I fought battle-weariness.

I had written in my journal of a challenging day, when out of aggravation, I had said to Mother, "I can't take this anymore!" She replied with complete composure, "Oh yes, you can!"

Even through the effects of dementia that hindered her ability to communicate, the Lord enabled Mother to speak spiritual truths to me with her simple, innocent responses. (Just another one of those things dementia couldn't steal.)

And, of course, she was right. I *could* continue, and did. I had just lost patience in the moment of a trying circumstance, likely compounded by a sequence of trying circumstances before that.

But by that time, I had listened to many friends throughout the years, when reflecting on the death of their parent(s), say something like, "Given another chance, I'd do *more* for them…not less." This was a powerful reminder for me of the limited-time opportunity I had to be a blessing to my mother—and why it was so important that I learned to stand in the victory that Jesus had already won for me.

Everything we need for victory is in Him—He desires to reveal His strength to us (2 Chronicles 16:9), and He has made us *more* than conquerors (Romans 8:37). We even have Jesus and the Holy Spirit interceding for us:

> *"Likewise the Spirit also helps in our weaknesses. For we do not know what we should pray for as we ought, but the Spirit Himself makes intercession for us with groanings which cannot be uttered. Now He who searches the hearts knows what the mind of the Spirit is, because He makes intercession for the saints according to the will of God. ... If God is for us, who can be against us? He who did not spare His own Son, but delivered Him up for us all, how shall He not with Him also freely give us all things? Who shall*

bring a charge against God's elect? It is God who justifies. Who is he who condemns? It is Christ who died, and furthermore is also risen, who is even at the right hand of God, who also makes intercession for us."

— Romans 8:26–27, 31–34, NKJV

If today you are in a battle, be of good cheer and confess these scriptural assurances of your victory from the Lord:

- *"My help comes from the Lord, Who made heaven and earth"* (Psalm 121:2, NKJV).
- *"Have I not commanded you? Be strong and of good courage; do not be afraid, nor be dismayed, for the Lord your God is with you wherever you go"* (Joshua 1:9, NKJV).
- *"So then, surrender to God. Stand up to the devil and resist him and he will flee in agony"* (James 4:7, TPT).
- *"But let all those rejoice who put their trust in You; Let them ever shout for joy, because You defend them; Let those also who love Your name Be joyful in You. For You, O Lord, will bless the righteous; With favor You will surround him as with a shield"* (Psalm 5:11–12, NKJV).
- *"For here is what the Lord has spoken to me: 'Because you loved me, delighted in me, and have been loyal to my name, I will greatly protect you. I will answer your cry for help every time you pray, and you will feel my presence in your time of trouble. I will deliver you and bring you honor. I will satisfy you with a full life and with all that I do for you. For you will enjoy the fullness of my salvation!'"* (Psalm 91:14–16, TPT).

- *"You see, every child of God overcomes the world, for our faith is the victorious power that triumphs over the world. So who are the world conquerors, defeating its power? Those who believe that Jesus is the Son of God"* (1 John 5:4–5, TPT).

Reflection and Application

Take a few minutes to read through Psalm 91 and Romans 8. Meditate on God's provision for your victory, and ask the Holy Spirit to increase your understanding of these powerful passages of Scripture.

Write a testimony about a battle that the Lord won for you. If you can't think of anything at this time, ask the Holy Spirit for wisdom on how to worship and pray through to victory in a current battle you are facing, and don't forget to write your testimony when your faith becomes sight!

Prayer of Declaration

> *Heavenly Father, I am grateful to know that my victories come from You, and that Jesus and the Holy Spirit are interceding for me in accordance with Your will. I submit to You and resist the devil—he must flee according to Your Word! Help me to testify of Your victories so that others may be strengthened in their faith. In all these things, may You receive the glory.*
> *In the name of Jesus, I pray. Amen.*

Day 20—Prosper in Covenant

"Blessed is the man Who walks not in the counsel of the ungodly, Nor stands in the path of sinners, Nor sits in the seat of the scornful; But his delight is in the law of the Lord, And in His law he meditates day and night. He shall be like a tree Planted by the rivers of water, That brings forth its fruit in its season, Whose leaf also shall not wither; And whatever he does shall prosper."

— Psalm 1:1–3, NKJV

Prosperity is a blessing of the Lord! It brings God delight to see His people prosper. King David wrote about it in a psalm: *"And let them say continually, 'Let the Lord be magnified, Who has pleasure in the prosperity of His servant'"* (Psalm 35:27, NKJV).

The blessing of prosperity is part of God's covenant with His people. Deuteronomy 8:18 (NKJV) says, *"And you shall remember the Lord your God, for it is He who gives you power to get wealth, that He may establish His covenant which He swore to your fathers, as it is this day."*

Prosperity and generosity go hand-in-hand for the believer. We are blessed to be a blessing! Everyone can have a generous heart and give to others, but with prosperity, one is afforded the joy of giving in greater measure and on a wider scale. It is so beautiful to experience the privilege of sharing with another the abundance the Lord has provided!

And, of course, it's always good to have funds available for unexpected major expenses, as I found out.

During the last few years Mother was with me, there were periods in which we needed round-the-clock caregiving assistance at home. I quickly realized that the expenses for salaries, taxes, and associated costs were significantly higher than I had expected—about twice as much as a nearby nursing home had quoted. Thankfully, we had sufficient funds in savings and some residual income to cover costs, but still I had to trust in the Lord, as I had no idea how long that season of high costs would last.

My experience in the area of finances has consistently been this: as I am faithful to honor God by stewarding the resources He has provided in a manner consistent with His Word, He has been faithful to pour out blessing upon blessing. When it is settled in our heart that God is our Provider —and not the entities from which funds may come our way —we can truly rest in His sufficiency. We have a scriptural promise that He supplies all our need (Philippians 4:19).

In Malachi 3:10 (NKJV), we are instructed to: *"'Bring all the tithes into the storehouse, That there may be food in My house,*

And try Me now in this,' Says the Lord of hosts, 'If I will not open for you the windows of heaven And pour out for you such blessing that there will not be room enough to receive it.'" Having followed this guidance for much of my adult life, I can testify He is faithful! He even gave me a special testimony about tithing.

I was still working during the first few years Mother was with me. At a certain point, I had heard someone teach about tithing in faith when believing for God's favor for promotion or a pay increase. So, I decided to pray for His blessing and increase my tithe amount.

At the time, I didn't look to see what the next level higher salary would be to determine my new tithe amount. I instead rounded up a bit to an even number, somewhat higher than what I was currently tithing. Of course, a tithe typically doesn't work out to an even number, and I had no idea what the actual new tithe amount would be if I were to get a pay raise—I just wanted to do something tangible to activate my faith and let the Lord know that I trusted in His provision.

Though I don't recall the exact duration of my faith tithing, I believe it was a period of months, perhaps about a year or so. When faith became sight, I recorded this joy-filled journal entry: "I received an unexpected (pay) increase this pay period! Amazing, as I went to recalculate my new tithe, it worked out to the exact figure I had been tithing! I had been paying over my tithe and the Lord grew my salary to match! Praise Him!"

Never doubt the generosity of the Lord. I've heard it said many times that you can't outgive God. In my experience, that has proven true!

My prayer for you, dear caregiver: May you prosper in every area of life, all the while offering your praise to our wonderful, generous Heavenly Father.

> *"Beloved friend, I pray that you are prospering in every way and that you continually enjoy good health, just as your soul is prospering."*
>
> — 3 John 1:2, TPT

Reflection and Application

In what ways are you enjoying the Lord's blessing of prosperity in your life (financial or otherwise)? Choose one of those blessings and ask the Lord for one step you can take to best steward it today to bring Him glory and joy.

Prayer of Declaration

> *Heavenly Father, I am so grateful for Your blessing of prosperity! Thank You for supplying all my need! I desire to reflect Your generous ways in my interactions with others, and I commit to managing the resources You have so bountifully supplied in a way that pleases You and accomplishes Your purposes. In the name of Jesus, I pray. Amen.*

Day 21—Divine Health

"But He was wounded for our transgressions, He was bruised for our iniquities; The chastisement for our peace was upon Him, And by His stripes we are healed."

— Isaiah 53:5, NKJV

CARING for a loved one can seem exponentially more difficult when you're not feeling well. And then there are times when the challenges of caregiving threaten to overwhelm your own self-care endeavors, further hindering your efforts to sustain optimal health. That's a vicious cycle best avoided...but how? Choose to contend in prayer and declaration of God's Word for divine health every day! Building a solid foundation on biblical truths strengthens your ability to maintain a dynamic faith to believe for a divinely healthy life.

Ready to get started? Let's dive into God's Word and soak it in!

In today's Scripture, the prophet Isaiah had recorded the pronouncement of healing by the stripes of the coming Messiah. The declaration was a prophetic one. It wasn't until after Jesus came to earth, took stripes on his body for our healing, and completed His work of redemption that the apostle Peter would write, *"by His stripes we were healed"* (1 Peter 2:24). A significant distinction with a compelling message—the price for our healing has been *fully* paid by our Savior!

We know that Jesus *"went about doing good and <u>healing all</u> who were oppressed by the devil"* (Acts 10:38, NKJV, emphasis added). When a healing occurred, Jesus often commended the *healed one* for their faith, even attributing the healing to it. Conversely, when healing did not manifest, Jesus cited unbelief: *"'A prophet is treated with honor everywhere except in his own hometown, among his relatives, and in his own house.' He was unable to do any great miracle in Nazareth, except to heal a few sick people by laying his hands upon them. He was <u>amazed at the depth of their unbelief</u>!"* (Mark 6:4–6, TPT, emphasis added).

Jesus did not allow people with unbelief to be nearby when He prayed for the daughter of Jairus, who had died (Luke 8:40–56). And when He was preparing to pray for the blind man at Bethsaida, He first led the man outside of his village (Mark 8:22–26). Even so, the man's sight—though restored fully—came back in stages, indicating some form of unbelief at work to impede the full manifestation of healing.

In this fallen world, with warfare being waged in the spirit realm, we must stand with determination on God's Word and fight from a position of victory, which Jesus has already secured for us! This will require us to fix our eyes on Him as the Author and Finisher of our faith (Hebrews 12:2), and not on the circumstances as they appear. He has given us His Word as a powerful weapon, the sword of the Spirit, and we must use it wisely.[1]

We know God's will by His Word, and these Scriptures pertaining to health and healing will help you get started in prayer. Faith comes by hearing, so I encourage you to read these verses out loud.

- *"My son, give attention to my words; Incline your ear to my sayings. Do not let them depart from your eyes; Keep them in the midst of your heart; For they are life to those who find them, And health to all their flesh"* (Proverbs 4:20–22, NKJV).
- *"Beloved friend, I pray that you are prospering in every way and that you continually enjoy good health, just as your soul is prospering"* (3 John 1:2, TPT).
- *"So you shall serve the Lord your God, and He will bless your bread and your water. And I will take sickness away from the midst of you"* (Exodus 23:25, NKJV).
- *"He sent His word and healed them, And delivered them from their destructions"* (Psalm 107:20, NKJV).
- *"I shall not die, but live, And declare the works of the Lord"* (Psalm 118:17, NKJV).
- *"With long life I will satisfy him, And show him My salvation."* (Psalm 91:16, NKJV).
- *"...I will fulfill the number of your days"* (Exodus 23:26, NKJV).

If you are feeling weary from a persistent health challenge you or a loved one are facing, take heart and meditate on the excruciating and incomprehensible cost Jesus already paid for your healing to manifest. Consider such love that would motivate the King of kings to put your weaknesses upon Himself and carry away your diseases (Matthew 8:17, TPT).

Reflection and Application

Are you or a loved one in need of healing? Apply healing Scriptures to your thoughts, and picture yourself or your loved one fully healed by the stripes of Jesus. Read through the Scriptures mentioned above, and others you find in God's Word, and declare them aloud over your situation. Thank the Lord for His finished work of healing and for imparting faith to you to believe for and see healing manifest, in yourself and others.[2]

Prayer of Declaration

> *Heavenly Father, thank You for Your provision for my every need, including healing, and the faith to believe for it. I declare in accordance with Your Word that by the stripes of Christ I was and am healed, and no weapon formed against me will prosper. I receive Your blessing to walk in divine health and Your promise of long life and strength for all my days—for myself and my loved ones. In the name of Jesus, I pray. Amen.*

Part Five

Giving

"*Give generously and generous gifts will be given back to you, shaken down to make room for more. Abundant gifts will pour out upon you with such an overflowing measure that it will run over the top! The measurement of your generosity becomes the measurement of your return.*"

— Luke 6:38, TPT

Day 22—Sowing and Reaping

"For what you plant will always be the very thing you harvest. The harvest you reap reveals the seed that was planted. ... And don't allow yourselves to be weary or disheartened in planting good seeds, for the season of reaping the wonderful harvest you've planted is coming! Take advantage of every opportunity to be a blessing to others, especially to our brothers and sisters in the family of faith!"

— Galatians 6:7–10, TPT

Our pastor had just preached an insightful sermon on the subject of reaping a harvest. As the service ended, my attention drifted to the typical after-church conversations, and then I was introduced to a new acquaintance.

I began to share, as I often did when meeting a new friend, that I was caring for my elderly mother at home. Being a caregiver had become such a part of my identity that I felt compelled to go through the story each time I was introduced to someone.

I would tell them about how I was not the "caregiver-type," and had never planned to be a stay-at-home daughter, but felt the Lord had prepared me for it…and so on.

My new friend graciously listened, and when I got to the part about how, though I was not a caregiver, my mother *had been*… Suddenly, as though the Lord had quickened to her a revelation from the sermon, her face lit up, and she exclaimed, "*You're* your mother's *harvest!*"

Me?! My mother's harvest?! I pondered, "Can a person become a harvest?"

It took a few moments for me to fully comprehend this insight my new friend had just revealed. The idea of it was astounding to me. I could hardly find words to respond, other than to smile and say how beautiful it was.

My mother was enjoying the benefits of a plentiful harvest from sowing caregiving seeds throughout her life. Though she only had one living child who had been staunchly career-focused and averse to the idea of providing personal care… and though it appeared she was destined to spend her elder years in a nursing facility (if she were to need care)—my mother's actions of ministering care to those in need served as seed sown that produced a crop according to its own kind.

In this case, the crop came in the form of a daughter to serve as her caregiver, enabling her to remain at home as she so dearly desired!

Jerry Savelle is one of my favorite Bible teachers, and he tells a story like no other. In an illustration I've heard him share about sowing and reaping, he recalls a time years ago of flying his plane to visit his friend and fellow minister, Charles Capps.

As Brother Jerry tells it, Charles was also a pilot and had cut a grass landing strip through the middle of his farm. Coming in for a landing, Jerry would pass between white fields of cotton lining both sides of the runway.

But one day as Jerry landed, there was no cotton…only a crop Jerry didn't recognize. He asked Charles why there was no cotton in the field. "Because I didn't want cotton," Charles quipped.

Jerry questioned further. "What did you plant?"

"Soybeans," Charles said. "Do you have any more luggage?"

Jerry persisted, "Why did you plant soybeans?"

"Because I wanted soybeans," Charles said, continuing. "Do you have any more luggage?"

As Brother Jerry explained, he had a revelation that day. "If you don't want cotton," he said, "don't plant cotton."[1] A farmer plants seeds to produce the crop he expects to harvest.

Similarly, though Mother didn't realize she was "planting" seeds of caring that would one day produce a harvest for her to enjoy, the biblical principle of sowing and reaping, nonetheless, worked. After spending much of my adult life convinced I would never be a caregiver, I became my mother's harvest.

Reflection and Application

What seeds are you sowing in life? Picture your harvest. Is it the harvest you desire? If so, continue sowing good seeds! If not, consider how you can begin to sow seeds that will produce the bountiful harvest you desire.

Ask the Lord. He is the one who supplies seed to the sower. And don't forget to thank Him for your harvest!

Prayer of Declaration

> *Heavenly Father, I desire to sow generously of the good seed You supply. Lead me to fertile soil, and give me a vision of the harvest You desire for me. Thank You for a bountiful harvest! In the name of Jesus, I pray. Amen.*

Day 23—Give

> "I've left you an example of how you should serve and take care of those who are weak. For we must always cherish the words of our Lord Jesus, who taught, 'Giving brings a far greater blessing than receiving.'"
>
> — Acts 20:35, TPT

All of us who belong to Jesus should be cheerful givers! It is such a blessing to bless someone else, and we know we're cherishing the Words of the Lord when we give.

We learn from our lead Scripture today that the Lord Jesus had said it's more blessed to give than to receive. So, we understand that it is, indeed, a blessing to receive…and yet a greater blessing to give.

Did you know you can prevent a giver from receiving a blessing if you do not receive their gift? Sometimes when I've given a gift, the person receiving the gift will say, "Thank you!" and I reply, "Thank you for *receiving*!" They are blessing me by receiving my gift, because they are enabling the blessing of the Lord to flow into my life. If no one receives, the giver is prevented from giving, and perhaps hindered from receiving a blessing even though they fully desired to give!

As busy caregivers, it can be tempting to turn our gaze inward and think that we're already giving so much (of our time, energy, and perhaps even finances), that there isn't anything left to give out. I believe that is a lie from the enemy that can result in stolen blessings. In my experience, the Lord enabled me to engage in various opportunities to give, even during my years of caregiving. I always felt His blessing through added purpose to my life and the personal satisfaction of partnering with others to accomplish things I could never have done on my own.

There certainly is no shortage of worthwhile causes needing our gifts. I have learned to seek God's guidance regarding where He wants me to devote my time and resources (His gifts to me). It has been said and I can testify, "Where God guides, He provides."

I've also experienced taking on something I didn't really feel He was leading me to do. Trying to make it work without His grace convinced me of the better way—seek first His guidance.

Many of us, meaning well, will readily declare our passion for a cause—such as feeding the hungry—but the true test of our sincerity is revealed in the degree to which we invest our time and resources toward the solution. It's always easier to point out what *others* should be doing. But complaining about a perceived lack of action on someone else's part is actually wasted time and energy—and may even equate to sowing seeds of discord.

So, let's commit to putting action to our convictions and focusing on ways we can help.

Solution #1: Tithe

The Word tells us that we are to: *"'Bring all the tithes into the storehouse, <u>That there may be food in My house</u>, And try Me now in this,' Says the Lord of hosts, 'If I will not open for you the windows of heaven And pour out for you such blessing That there will not be room enough to receive it'"* (Malachi 3:10, NKJV, emphasis added).

Tithing is part of God's solution to feed the hungry. Many churches have their own food pantry and/or support local food banks or international relief organizations. That's a great place to start. And tithing comes with the added promise of God's blessing in a greater measure than we can even receive!

Solution #2: Partner with fellow believers

Churches and ministries that send individuals and teams locally, or even around the world to help with meeting needs and spreading the Gospel, are always in need of partners who will pray and assist through financial gifts. Some can go, and some can send (either funds or prayer support to enable others to go and physically do the work). This can be a very meaningful way to contribute to a worthy cause. And in God's equation, both the goer and the sender share in the reward!

> "Forsake the habit of criticizing and judging others, and you will not be criticized and judged in return. Don't condemn others and you will not be condemned. Forgive over and over, and you will be forgiven over and over. Give generously and generous gifts will be given back to you, shaken down to make room for more. Abundant gifts will pour out upon you with such an overflowing measure that it will run over the top! The measurement of your generosity becomes the measurement of your return."
>
> — Luke 6:37–38, TPT

Reflection and Application

Consider an issue that matters to you, whether that may be hunger, human trafficking, poverty, or another problem needing a solution. Pray and ask the Holy Spirit for one action of personal giving (prayer, volunteering, donations, and/or partnership with a ministry) that you can take today to become part of the solution.

Prayer of Declaration

> *Heavenly Father, You have blessed me greatly, and I desire to steward my life and resources to bring You glory. Please illuminate to me the ways that I am pleasing You in my giving, and also any areas of potential blessing that I have yet to step into. Help me to be like You in abundant generosity. In the name of Jesus, I pray. Amen.*

Day 24—The Gift of Forgiveness

"Forgive us the wrongs we have done as we ourselves release forgiveness to those who have wronged us."

— Matthew 6:12, TPT

Forgiveness is one of the most powerful healing substances on earth, I am convinced! It was significant enough for Jesus to include in His model prayer, as we read in Matthew 6:12. How could we ever withhold a gift from another that we ourselves have so graciously received from the Lord (Acts 10:43)?

Especially when that gift is one we, ourselves, receive when we give.

Think of the immeasurable price Jesus paid to atone for the sin of mankind—His precious blood. He offers forgiveness freely to *all* who will receive Him. Jesus lived a sinless life and took the punishment that each of us deserved. The burden of judging the living and the dead has been appointed to Him by the Father (Acts 10:42); He alone is the righteous Judge (2 Timothy 4:8).

How do you forgive what feels unforgivable, some ask. By faith, in obedience, and with an awareness that our emotions may not perfectly align with our decision. Understanding that up front helps so that we aren't tempted to question or withdraw our choice to forgive.

God's Word doesn't instruct us to wait for some emotional cue to discern the opportune time "when" or "if" to forgive. Nor is forgiveness on our part a determination of innocence on someone else's. By choosing to forgive, we are releasing judgment for an offense into God's capable hands, which is the only place that judgment rightly belongs.

This step of faith sets the forgiver on the path of liberation from an offense, while unforgiveness imprisons one in bondage to it. Feelings may sway to-and-fro, but abiding in obedience to God's commands releases freedom and healing into our lives.

If that were not reason enough to choose forgiveness, the Lord offers a stern warning of dire consequences awaiting those who fail to forgive. In Matthew 6:14–15 (TPT), Jesus said, *"For if you forgive men their trespasses, your heavenly Father will also forgive you. But if you do not forgive men their trespasses, neither will your Father forgive your trespasses."*

Consider these undesirable outcomes associated with unforgiveness:

- Unforgiveness puts one in direct disobedience to God's Word.

- Unforgiveness perpetuates bondage to the offense.
- Unforgiveness shackles the offended one with the burden of judgment—a responsibility they were not designed to bear.
- Unforgiveness hinders prayer and impedes the flow of God's mercy into the offended one's life.

Contrast the above to these beneficial attributes of forgiveness. You may want to read these aloud, as a personal declaration:

- Forgiveness is my choice in obedience to God's Word.
- Forgiveness frees me from the burden of judging another, and it properly places the burden of judgment on Jesus, as the Father has appointed.
- Forgiveness releases God's forgiveness for my sins.
- Forgiveness removes hindrances from my prayers.
- Forgiveness is life-giving! Through my obedience, Christ sets me free indeed (John 8:36).

As Mother's caregiver, the most difficult moments of maintaining my typically peaceful demeanor came when dementia symptoms would cause her to act contrary to her own gentle nature…or when I was feeling weary and overwhelmed. While I wish my words would have always been spoken in compassion, in the times when I lost my patience or responded in an unkind tone of voice, I swiftly sought forgiveness from the Lord and Mother.

Assured of the Lord's forgiveness (1 John 1:9), what surprised me was my mother's reaction. Even if, moments before, we had been in conflict or discord, she would consistently respond to my request for forgiveness *as if no offense had occurred,* saying, "I think you're the best person in the world!" or "I think you're perfect!"

Admittedly, I never felt very close to achieving perfection as a caregiver, but Mother always knew I was trying to do my best for her. In her eyes, I was her "perfect" caregiver—*even with my failures.*

Though the thief of dementia had stolen from her, she was a living testament to a precious commodity it could not steal— the ability to reflect the love of the Lord Jesus by offering the gift of forgiveness. And in giving, she also received.

Reflection and Application

If you struggle with letting go of offenses and offering forgiveness, pray and ask the Holy Spirit to help you to release any and all burdens that you were not designed or assigned to carry. Study the Scriptures dealing with forgiveness in the Bible. Here are a few to help you get started: Ephesians 4:32, Colossians 3:12–13, Matthew 18:21–35.

Read Mark 11:25–26, and put it into practice before praying the Prayer of Declaration below. Consider that it will always be in your best interest to live in an attitude of forgiveness. If a thought comes to mind of something you could carry as an offense, even if you've already forgiven, immediately pray and release it to the Lord, thanking Him for your freedom!

Prayer of Declaration

Father in Heaven, I praise You for the blessing that is mine when I obey Your Word! I am grateful for the gift of forgiveness. I commit myself to obedience in forgiving every offense, and I'm thankful to know You are my ever-present Help in the times when doing so is a challenge. The desire of my heart is to live in obedience to Your Word.
In the name of Jesus, I pray. Amen.

Day 25—Be a Wonder-Worker: Encourage

"Anxious fear brings depression, but a life-giving word of encouragement can do <u>wonders</u> to restore joy to the heart."

— Proverbs 12:25, TPT (emphasis added)

In my experience, it isn't often that we are presented with an opportunity to do a "wonder." And yet that is exactly what our Scripture for today emphasizes: we possess the ability to speak an encouraging word.

You certainly don't have to look very far to find people who are discouraged, stressed, or feeling unappreciated. I see them every day—at the drive-through window when I'm picking up lunch, while I'm out doing errands, and even at church. It is such a joy to speak a kind word of encouragement and see someone's countenance visibly brighten as a smile comes to their face!

I have determined that part of my life's calling is to be an encourager, in large part because of the happiness it brings *me* to see this transformation in others. And as an encourager, I have a strong personal motivation to encourage others to be encouragers!

Here's what the apostle Paul said in his letter to the believers in Rome: *"Now, this means that when we come together and are side by side, something wonderful will be released. We can expect to be co-encouraged and co-comforted by each other's faith!"* (Romans 1:12, TPT).

The Lord has taught me so much in recent years about the power of encouragement—at, believe it or not, drive-through restaurants.

Whenever a caregiver came to be with Mother, I took daily respite trips to one of many nearby drive-throughs. Along with picking up meals to bring home, I looked forward to a refreshing cup of iced tea (my *comfort food*—half sweet/half unsweet with extra ice, in case you were wondering)!

These daily trips also afforded me a golden opportunity to interact with the folks who were working at the drive-through window.

Because I was driving through so frequently at certain restaurants, the staff members came to know me, and often several of them would come to the window to say hello when they saw me sitting there in my vehicle. Time being of the essence in a drive-through meant that I didn't have long to interact with the team members, but I would always try to offer a few words of encouragement along with a monetary tip to show my appreciation.

I now understand that, at a deeper level, I was affirming the significance of their work…and they responded so beautifully. Many of them knew of my situation with Mother, and I believe I was able to convey to them the importance of their efforts in providing a meal that I, as a weary caregiver, didn't have to cook.

An odd phenomenon began to occur—and has continued—in which the staff members began to show their appreciation to me in unusual ways. Many times, they wouldn't let me pay for my iced tea, even though I said I'd like to pay for it. At one restaurant, the young ladies would write sweet notes on the lid of my iced tea, like "We love you!" (complete with hearts). Once, as I pulled away from the pick-up window, I heard a young lady tell another girl, "Darlene was just here," and as I drove out of the lane, that young lady came running out the front door, waving and shouting, "Bye, Darlene!" They made me feel like royalty…and all because I made a simple effort to show my appreciation and encourage them.

One of my favorite stories is of a young man who helped me at a popular drive-through one afternoon. They were short-staffed, and the line of cars at this restaurant was often long. I should know—I was there at least three to four times a week. As I drove up to pay for my cheeseburger or whatever I had ordered that day, I asked the young man how he was doing. He said, "Oh, outstanding! I just got yelled at by the last eight customers!" (If that wasn't a perfect lead-in for an encourager at heart, I don't know what is!) So, with the next minute and a half or two that I had, I told him that I loved this restaurant and that, even short-handed, I thought they were doing a great job. I even said, "I wish I could come join the team and help you," to which he replied, "Oh, ma'am, we would love that!" He seemed visibly touched by my caring words after he had received the opposite from previous customers.

Your tongue holds the power of death and life (Proverbs 18:21). Want to be a wonder-worker? Speak life-giving words and encourage!

Reflection and Application

Do you actively look for ways to encourage others each day? Pray and ask the Lord to bring to your attention today one person who needs to hear an uplifting word. An easy way to start is to thank someone who has helped you at a restaurant or store. Observe their countenance and response to your words of appreciation and encouragement.

Prayer of Declaration

> *Heavenly Father, may my words be pleasing to You, and may they impart blessing to others. I ask that You would illuminate specific words of encouragement for me to speak that will minister joy to the hearts of those around me each day. Thank You for Holy Spirit promptings so that I won't miss any opportunities to share life-giving words. In the name of Jesus, I pray. Amen.*

Day 26—Cast Vision

"When there is no clear prophetic vision, people quickly wander astray. But when you follow the revelation of the Word, heaven's bliss fills your soul."

— Proverbs 29:18, TPT

Caregiver, have you taken hold of God's vision for your life? If so, what does it include? Certainly your service to your loved one, in and of itself, is a high calling. I would encourage you, however, not to let the intensity of a caregiving season dim your vision to additional purposes the Lord may have for you. His ability to accomplish through your life every divine plan He envisioned is in no way diminished due to the needs of your loved one.

Have you considered that part of God's plan for your life might be to encourage others to aspire to His vision for their lives?

I never expected during my caregiving years to become an encourager for drive-through restaurant workers, but I did and that continues to this day. I am now a firm believer in the importance of speaking blessings to and over others. And anyone can do that. We can all minister God's love to the person in front of us, whether to our loved one we're caring for, a friend…or even the person at the drive-through window!

While we're offering life-giving words, let's go a step further. Building upon yesterday's devotional reading, let us consider *casting vision* as one of the highest forms of encouragement.

When you cast vision for someone, you're inspiring them to take hold of a God-fashioned blueprint for their future. You're offering much more than a pep talk—you're kindling a calling to something of greater significance than they could ever conceive or achieve on their own. How wonderful to consider that *you could be the one* to help someone tap into a divine purpose for their life that may seem unlikely or even unattainable from their vantage point…that is, until they connect with the One with whom *nothing is impossible*.

Casting vision may take the form of encouraging a friend to consider an option that could change the trajectory of their life, or the sacred duty of helping our loved one envision their beautiful home in Heaven that they will blissfully enjoy for eternity—now, there's a divine vision no one should miss! In any case, consider what a privilege it is to come alongside another to help build anticipation for their future when so many other voices in life are invoking negativity or, at best, the status quo.

The first key to enabling another to pursue vision for their future is to help them *let go* of the past. How often have you seen someone continually remind another of their failures? That's painful to watch or experience. Let's choose instead to affirm the good they're doing.

I invite you to listen carefully as you read aloud this passage written by the apostle Paul:

> *"I admit that I haven't yet acquired the absolute fullness that I'm pursuing, but I run with passion into his abundance so that I may reach the purpose for which Christ Jesus laid hold of me to make me his own. I don't depend on my own strength to accomplish this; however I do have one compelling focus: I forget all of the past as I fasten my heart to the future instead. I run straight for the divine invitation of reaching the heavenly goal and gaining the victory-prize through the anointing of Jesus. So let all who are fully mature have this same passion, and if anyone is not yet gripped by these desires, God will reveal it to them. And let us all advance together to reach this victory-prize, following one path with one passion."*
>
> — Philippians 3:12–16, TPT

The principles in these verses apply to each of us and are also at work in those we influence. That's right. Every single one of us is an influencer in some way. With our words, we can empower others to leave the past behind and fasten their hearts to the future to attain heavenly goals.

Let's inspire others to fix their gaze ahead with high expectations. Celebrate their *successes.* In doing so, you're instilling confidence in them to believe and strive for greater achievement. Yes, be an encourager—and don't stop there. Cast vision for what our all-powerful Heavenly Father can accomplish through a yielded vessel. Your words could change someone's life for the better!

> *"Then the Lord answered me and said: 'Write the vision And make it plain on tablets, That he may run who reads it. For the vision is yet for an appointed time; But at the end it will speak, and it will not lie. Though it tarries, wait for it; Because it will surely come, It will not tarry.'"*
>
> — HABAKKUK 2:2–3, NKJV

Reflection and Application

What do you see in others? How often do you envision God-sized dreams for someone's life—things they could only accomplish with His help? How successful are you at affirming God-given giftings in others, including the loved one you care for? Pray and ask the Lord for a word of affirmation for another, and begin to cast vision into their life.

Prayer of Declaration

Heavenly Father, help me to be a vision caster!
Open my eyes to see the best in others, and illuminate Your divine plans and purposes for those around me so that I may encourage and affirm them. Help me to inspire others to activate the full measure of faith You've imparted so they can believe beyond their dreams to embrace Yours!
In the name of Jesus, I pray. Amen.

Part Six
Shining

"Live a cheerful life, without complaining or division among yourselves. For then you will be seen as innocent, faultless, and pure children of God, even though you live in the midst of a brutal and perverse culture. For you will appear among them as shining lights in the universe, holding out the words of eternal life."

— Philippians 2:14–16, TPT

Day 27—Gaze Upon Him and Shine

"You are the light of the world. A city that is set on a hill cannot be hidden. Nor do they light a lamp and put it under a basket, but on a lampstand, and it gives light to all who are in the house. Let your light so shine before men, that they may see your good works and glorify your Father in heaven."

— Matthew 5:14–16, NKJV

You have the wonderful privilege, dear caregiver, of letting your light shine! In doing so, you bless your loved one and those around you, particularly as they see you shining in a situation that could appear clouded, if not for the Light of the Lord. Your cheerful countenance through any circumstance is evidence of His Light shining through you.

The apostle Paul offers insight and direction for us on the topic of shining: *"Live a cheerful life, without complaining or division among yourselves. For then you will be seen as innocent, faultless, and pure children of God, even though you live in the midst of a brutal and perverse culture. For you will appear among them as shining lights in the universe, holding out the words of eternal life"* (Philippians 2:14–16, TPT).

Though there are times when we may not feel like shining, nothing can stand against a believer's scriptural mandate to let their light shine. No power of darkness sent from the enemy can dim the light of a believer who is filled with the light of life, infused by the Light of the World. With Christ in us, the hope of glory (Colossians 1:27), we shine supernaturally!

"Then Jesus spoke to them again, saying, 'I am the light of the world. He who follows Me shall not walk in darkness, but have the light of life'" (John 8:12, NKJV). As you follow Jesus, you *will* have the light of life. There is no on-off switch as long as you are abiding in Him.

> *"Once your life was full of sin's darkness, but now you have the very light of our Lord shining through you because of your union with him. Your mission is to live as children flooded with his revelation-light! And the supernatural fruits of his light will be seen in you—goodness, righteousness, and truth. Then you will learn to choose what is beautiful to our Lord."*
>
> — Ephesians 5:8–10, TPT

Along with keeping your own light brightly shining, while you care for your loved one, remember that they also have a light that needs to shine! With your encouragement and the Lord's enablement, through any difficulty—even if they are passing through the valley of the shadow of death—their light need not fade.

As we read in John 1:4–5 (TPT), *"A fountain of life was in him, for his life is light for all humanity. And this Light never fails to shine through darkness—Light that darkness could not overcome!"*

Mother loved the Gaither Music Homecoming videos, and she always wanted me right there enjoying the music with her! She particularly loved their Gospel Bluegrass programs,[1] as she grew up around bluegrass and country music. It is such a comfort to the elderly when you share with them the music of their youth!

One of Mother's favorites was the old song "This Little Light of Mine."[2] She would clap and sing along, and even play the "air" banjo with the musicians! If you weren't feeling the joy of the Lord before you entered her room, you would be soon.

Mother let her light shine brightly, and it brought joy to so many, including me! The joy of the Lord in her was contagious and would bless her caregivers and other visitors to our home. Though the effects of dementia and sickness were set against her shining, they couldn't extinguish her light. Even in the hours before Mother passed into Glory, her light still shone.

One of my pastors who came to visit said that she sensed the peace and presence of the Lord in Mother's room so strongly that she later told her husband, our senior pastor, "That's how it *always* should be!"

Keep your gaze on His beautiful face, and shine His light!

> "For God, who said, 'Let brilliant light shine out of darkness,' is the one who has cascaded his light into us—the brilliant dawning light

of the glorious knowledge of God as we gaze into the face of Jesus Christ."

— 2 CORINTHIANS 4:6, TPT

REFLECTION AND APPLICATION

In what ways does your life reflect (shine) the Light of the Lord to others?

Meditate on Ephesians 5:8–10. Ask the Lord how you are doing on your mission to live flooded with His revelation-light. Seek an opportunity today to shine more brightly for Him.

PRAYER OF DECLARATION

Heavenly Father, thank You for giving us Jesus as the Light of the World and for creating us as bearers of His light that cannot be overcome by darkness. Make my light, and the light of my dear one, shine brightly for You, so that others will see, be drawn to You, and give You glory! In the name of Jesus, I pray. Amen.

Day 28—Reflect the Fruit of the Spirit

> *"But the fruit of the Spirit is love, joy, peace, longsuffering, kindness, goodness, faithfulness, gentleness, self-control. Against such there is no law. And those who are Christ's have crucified the flesh with its passions and desires. If we live in the Spirit, let us also walk in the Spirit."*
>
> — Galatians 5:22–25, NKJV

What we reflect (shine) through our countenance, words, and actions has a distinct impact on those around us—and testifies of our relationship with the Lord. As believers, we desire to be a blessing to others and to reflect (and represent) the Lord in a way that honors and bears fruit for Him.

I often speak of my gratitude for the team of caregivers and helpers who came alongside to assist during the challenging late stages of Mother's care. Some became like family to us as they served in the love of the Lord. I've included remembrances of these dear "sisters"[1] alongside our lead Scripture passage from Galatians 5:22–23 (TPT), which beautifully ascribes actions to the virtues.

But the fruit produced by the Holy Spirit within you is divine love *in all its varied expressions*:

- joy *that overflows* (Abigail consistently brought the joy of the Lord into our home by her cheerful countenance, sweetly serenading Mother through the day in word and song),
- peace *that subdues* (Salome radiated peace from her absolute trust in the Lord that quickly subdued any turmoil or upsetting circumstance),
- patience *that endures* (Naomi consistently exhibited patience rooted in love through many challenging situations, always giving honor to Mother and protecting her dignity),
- kindness *in action* (Ruth's kindness overflowed as she provided Mother with unique opportunities for communicating through dementia with activities that added creative purpose to her life; Johanna was a gift, choosing to forego a salary to instead share her kindness and love with us as a volunteer),
- a life full of virtue (Elise imparted multi-faceted virtues and goodness in her provision of blessings—showering us with gifts, tangible and intangible, that continue to this day),
- faith *that prevails* (Evelyn's prevailing prayer-warrior faith was inspirational to me so that my own faith was strengthened),
- gentleness *of heart* (Annie's sweet and gentle spirit shone through her every word and deed, and was a

great comfort in the weeks and days surrounding Mother's homegoing),
- and strength *of spirit* (Christine and Sarah displayed strength through their dependability, which greatly blessed me, and personal dedication to providing exceptional care for Mother).

More than anything else I've experienced in life, caregiving regularly presented me with opportunities to display the fruit of the Spirit. My flesh, on the other hand, demanded a competing response. Though I desired to always respond in alignment with the Spirit's fruit, I learned that my own strength was insufficient to help me do so consistently in some of the intensely challenging situations that I faced.

I couldn't produce fruitfulness by striving in my own works —and neither can you. It springs forth from *abiding*: *"So you must remain in life-union with me, for I remain in life-union with you. For as a branch severed from the vine will not bear fruit, so your life will be fruitless unless you live your life intimately joined to mine. I am the sprouting vine and you're my branches. As you live in union with me as your source, fruitfulness will stream from within you—but when you live separated from me you are powerless"* (John 15:4–5, TPT).

What a relief! No more struggling to be good enough or fretting that we aren't good enough. It's as simple as abiding in Christ to reap a harvest of fruitfulness.

But wait—it gets better. Have you ever felt you weren't producing much fruit or even like a fruitless branch that deserved to be tossed out? I have. The good news is that is *not* how God sees us, as long as we abide in Him! As Jesus explained in John 15:1–2 (TPT): *"I am a true sprouting vine, and the farmer who tends the vine is my Father. He cares for the branches connected to me by lifting and propping up the fruitless branches and pruning every fruitful branch to yield a greater harvest."*

The only branches that will be tossed into the fire and burned are the ones who are separated from Jesus (John 15:6). As long as we remain in Him, we have His promise of fruitfulness.

So, the next time you need a countenance lifter to help you shine forth the fruit of the Spirit, remember that you *already have* a Divine Helper: *"Hope in God; For I shall yet praise Him, The help of my countenance and my God"* (Psalm 42:11, NKJV).

In Him is all you need—in every situation, at all times! Abide in Him and behold His work in you to produce an ever brighter reflection of the fruit of His Spirit streaming from within.

REFLECTION AND APPLICATION

Ask yourself: What is shining today through my countenance, words, and actions? Am I looking upon Jesus and reflecting Him through Christlike character?

For inspiration on how the Lord enables you to shine for Him, meditate on this verse: *"We can all draw close to him with the veil removed from our faces. And with no veil we all become like mirrors who brightly reflect the glory of the Lord Jesus. We are being transfigured into his very image as we move from one brighter level of glory to another. And this glorious transfiguration comes from the Lord, who is the Spirit"* (2 Corinthians 3:18, TPT).

Pray and ask the Lord to help you draw closer to Him today and abide there more completely.

Focus on His Spirit producing fruit on the inside of you, reflected on the outside, as you go through your day. Give Him praise!

Prayer of Declaration

Heavenly Father, thank You for Your ever-present help so that my countenance will always reflect the fruit of Your Spirit. Help me to more fully abide in You. I am so grateful to have Your Holy Spirit working in me to produce fruitfulness for Your glory! In the name of Jesus, I pray. Amen.

Day 29—Seek Divine Appointments—and Be One

"And God is able to make all grace abound toward you, that you, always having all sufficiency in all things, may have an abundance for every good work."

— 2 Corinthians 9:8, NKJV, emphasis added

Few things are as faith-building as a divine appointment… God's supernatural provision in His perfect timing! You know—that instance when you really need something to happen or an encouraging word—and it seems like the Lord brings just the right person into your life unexpectedly with precisely what you need to move forward.

Without divine appointments, I likely would not have had the courage to keep Mother at home. But God, in His providential wisdom, divinely brought people into my path over a period of many years before my caregiving season began. They inspired me by their selfless service to an elderly loved one (typically their mother or father). I found myself feeling deeply respectful of these people…to the point of wondering how they could love so greatly to do that. Their commitment to their loved one seemed so out of the ordinary. I reasoned that somehow I must be different. As much as I loved my mother, I could not comprehend making that kind of sacrifice, and honestly, I hoped it would be a decision I wouldn't ever have to make.

I now realize the Lord was using those divine appointments through the years to gently adjust my paradigm. With each family caregiver I met, He was softening my heart and preparing me to say "yes" to serve a precious lady who had poured her life into mine. The Lord was positioning me to keep Mother at home through her final and most vulnerable years of life, which was her heartfelt desire.

It is wonderful when God makes a divine appointment connection for you…and, oh, the satisfaction when He makes *you* the divine appointment for another.

One of my favorite testimonies is of a unique opportunity the Lord gave me to give through what I believe was a divine appointment. At my church, we often had "Acts 13" Missions luncheons on Sunday afternoons when missionaries would come to town and raise funds. I enjoyed the luncheons, but wasn't planning to attend this one. I didn't know the speakers, and though this was during the time when I felt comfortable leaving Mother alone for a short period, I typically went straight home after church to check on her.

After service that day, a lady and I were talking near the back of the sanctuary when the Missions pastor suddenly popped in through a door from the hallway, pointed at me, and with urgency and excitement in his voice, said, "Acts 13! Are you coming?!"

I muddled through the best answer I could muster, saying, "Well, I hadn't planned to... I *guess* I can go... I need to call Mother first and make sure she's okay."

He said with a smile, "Okay!" and disappeared back out the door as quickly as he had appeared. The odd thing was he didn't interact with the lady I was talking with at all. It was as if he felt I should be there.

I called Mother (at this time she could still take phone calls), and she said she was fine, that I should go ahead to the luncheon, so I made my way to the Fellowship Hall, letting the Missions pastor know I would be staying for the program.

After the meal, I listened as this couple spoke passionately about their mission field and their love for the people they would minister to. I found myself not just in tears but physically shaking and trying to hold back weeping sobs. The Lord was moving my heart in a powerful way, and I felt inspired to help this couple and their children get to their new ministry home.

I had just purchased a new home for Mother and myself, though we had not yet moved in. I had some funds saved up to update the kitchen, but God was showing me that He had better plans for that money! All I could think of was that I needed to donate those funds to help this family get to their mission field to share God's love with people desperate for it.

As it worked out, this family would be in town for a few extra days, so we were able to have lunch together, and they came to my new home. I showed them the kitchen that I had planned to remodel, which was functional and lovely in its current form, and said, "When I am in this kitchen, I'll pray for you and the people you are serving!" I asked them to pray over my new home, which they did, and soon thereafter they made the long journey to their new home.

The Lord gave us reciprocal blessings that day. Their prayers helped me establish my new household, and my giving helped them establish theirs. I wonder how many souls have been saved because of their obedience to go and my privilege to help send them. I am so grateful I didn't miss that divinely-appointed lunch date!

Reflection and Application

Pray and ask the Lord for a divine appointment today. Perhaps someone needs a word of encouragement, to hear that God loves them, or has a practical need you can help with.

After you've prayed, look for your opportunity! And don't be surprised if a divine appointment for blessing comes your way!

Prayer of Declaration

> *Heavenly Father, thank You for divine appointments for me to bless others. Order my steps that I may minister Your love and provision to those around me each day. How grateful I am for Your grace that abounds toward me, that You bless me with all*

sufficiency in all things for every good work. And when Your mercy leads someone my way to offer a divinely appointed blessing, I will receive it with gratitude and give You praise!
In the name of Jesus, I pray. Amen.

Day 30—Walking Homeward

"Though I walk through the valley of the shadow of death, I will fear no evil; For You are with me; Your rod and Your staff, they comfort me. ... Surely goodness and mercy shall follow me All the days of my life; And I will dwell in the house of the Lord Forever."

— Psalm 23:4, 6, NKJV

At one time or another, many of us have likely dreamt of our dream home. Perhaps only in our daydreams, but something deep inside yearns for that lovely sanctuary-haven abode, our personal oasis of refuge where everything is perfectly to our liking and desires, and where all dwell in peace and harmony. (Maybe you're picturing it now!)

Sounds heavenly, doesn't it?! How comforting to read in Scripture that Jesus is preparing a place for us. *"My Father's house has many dwelling places. If it were otherwise, I would tell you plainly, because I go to prepare a place for you. And when *everything is ready, I will come back and take you to myself so that you will be where I am"* (John 14:2–3, TPT).

Heaven is our forever "Dream Home"—fashioned by the Master Designer for those who love Him, and as I envision it, the crowning glory is His presence! The promise of it is glorious, such that every believer should look with great anticipation to the day we are transported to our forever Home. And I believe most do... There just seems to be a natural fear that we must overcome regarding the passage from here to there. However, we can take courage in the scriptural assurance that absence from our earthly bodies means presence with the Lord:

> *"For we know that if our earthly house, this tent, is destroyed, we have a building from God, a house not made with hands, eternal in the heavens. For in this we groan, earnestly desiring to be clothed with our habitation which is from heaven, if indeed, having been clothed, we shall not be found naked. ... We are confident, yes, well pleased rather to be absent from the body and to be present with the Lord."*
>
> — 2 Corinthians 5:1–3, 8, NKJV

As a caregiver, I felt that one of my highest callings was to help Mother prepare for her transition to her heavenly home. I wanted her to be ready, and totally free of fear, to depart this life for eternity with joy. I would encourage her often of the beauty of our heavenly home and the wonder of seeing Jesus face-to-face!

Oh, how she loved singing that old gospel chorus, "What a day that will be, when my Jesus I shall see! When I look upon

His face, the One who saved me by His grace. When He takes me by the hand, and leads me through the Promised Land, what a day—glorious day—that will be!"[1]

When she could no longer sing those words, we'd sit on the couch together, and I would sing for her. She would nod her head or tap my leg along with the music. Sometimes through tears, she would say, "Thank you!"

Those beautiful lyrics and melody brought comfort to both of us, as we imagined walking through the Promised Land with Jesus. It helped remind us that, while each day of our life on earth is a gift to be treasured, as the apostle Paul said in Philippians 1:23, it is *far better* to be in the presence of the Lord!

Before I became Mother's caregiver, I was a bit reluctant about the idea of walking someone through the final stages of their life here on earth. I had never gone through that experience with anyone before, and I didn't know what to expect. When fearful thoughts came, I had to stand on God's Word and take those thoughts captive to the obedience of Christ (2 Corinthians 10:5) in order to minister freedom and peace to my mother.

And while there were sorrows associated with our journey through that valley, I can now look back and say it was the privilege of a lifetime to hold her hand and walk with her Homeward. She seemed very comforted to have me close by during those final years, and I always tried to point her to Jesus—our ultimate Source of comfort.

I am so grateful that we were able to share remembrances of the beauty of our earthly lives that God had blessed us with, and look with wonder and anticipation to our heavenly home where there will be no more pain, no more tears, and no more death...but rather peace, joy, and worship-filled bliss, in the Presence of our King!

Reflection and Application

Think of your loved one's favorite hymns or songs about heaven and being with the Lord. Take time today to sing a song or two together. If you need help getting started, there are many hymns and gospel songs available to watch or listen to online. Make some beautiful memories as you reminisce about times gone by and look toward eternal life in your heavenly home with the Lord.

Prayer of Declaration

> *Heavenly Father, thank You for preparing a heavenly home for all who love You and for Your comforting presence with us! Help us to look ahead with great anticipation to dwelling with You for eternity, and thank You for blessing us with Your perfect love that casts out all fear. In the name of Jesus, I pray. Amen.*

Day 31—Letting Go and Going Forth

"As for us, we have all of these great witnesses who encircle us like clouds. So we must let go of every wound that has pierced us and the sin we so easily fall into. Then we will be able to run life's marathon race with passion and determination, for the path has been already marked out before us."

— Hebrews 12:1, TPT

Running your race means letting go of the past and moving toward a goal. As the apostle Paul said in Philippians 3:14, *"I press toward the goal for the prize of the upward call of God in Christ Jesus."*

On our journey through the seasons of life, we can expect unexpected hurdles, turns, and obstacles that we must maneuver around, over, or through. In times of bitter and sweet, as we fix our eyes on Jesus, the Author and Finisher of our faith (Hebrews 12:2), we are assured of reaching our goal.

Whether or not we've had time to prepare, a season of grief can challenge us like no other. As caregivers, we invest so much of our lives into our loved one, that when they go to be with the Lord, or somehow transition from our care, we can be left wondering, "What now?"

Receiving comfort, and keeping our thoughts focused on the Lord, helps us to move *through* a period of mourning to joy. While grieving is a natural phase in the healing process, getting stuck there will not produce fruit in our lives, nor will it bring our loved one back. It will hinder us from running the race God has marked out for us. There comes a time when we must release the past and go forward. Our hope remains in the Lord, and He has offered guidance and provision for passing through a season of grief:

- Draw near to the Lord and receive: *"The Spirit of the Lord God is upon Me ... He has sent Me to heal the brokenhearted ... To comfort all who mourn ... To give them beauty for ashes, The oil of joy for mourning, The garment of praise for the spirit of heaviness ... that He may be glorified"* (Isaiah 61:1–3, NKJV).
- Allow the Lord and others to comfort you: *"Blessed are those who mourn, For they shall be comforted"* (Matthew 5:4, NKJV).
- Gaze upon Jesus, and don't look away: *"You will keep him in perfect peace, Whose mind is stayed on You, Because he trusts in You"* (Isaiah 26:3, NKJV).

I experienced most of my grieving during Mother's last weeks, particularly in the days before she passed. I couldn't tell if she was uncomfortable, I wasn't sure what to do to comfort her, and the uncertainty of it all was upsetting. When it was apparent that she could no longer speak, she assured me of her enduring love and care by squeezing my hand as I wept by her bedside. And then, a special gift… She said, "I love you, Darlene," and it soothed my grieving heart.

About a month following Mother's homegoing, I wrote the closing entry in my journal: "I've started my new journal today as I'm working to close the old season and move into the new. This eleven years of having Mother with me has been the most significant time in my life, I believe. I've often thanked the Lord for the 'beautiful and terrible privilege' because it has been both and more! I miss Mother, but am left with deep peace and gratefulness. Peace and joy to think of her with the Lord in Heaven, and overflowing gratefulness to know the Lord enabled me to persevere and keep her home till He called her Home—as He showed me in a dream years ago. So thankful that I can now declare: 'It was worth it all!'"

As a friend recently shared, it was as if I was stating, "This chapter is now *closed*." My caregiving season completed, I had come through with a testimony. Though much bitter had accompanied the sweet during those years, the Lord in His goodness always made the sweet outshine the bitter.

Since that time, the Lord guided me through a peaceful transition, including two cross-country moves with an extended respite in the Land of my Heart (Arizona) and a return after many years to my home state of Florida. Now, as I embark upon a new season, He has blessed me with the opportunity to write this devotional, fulfilling a calling and desire of my heart since my caregiving days, in the hope of offering comfort and inspiration to caregivers.

> *"But we run our race to win a victor's crown that will last forever."*
>
> — 1 Corinthians 9:25, TPT

Reflection and Application

Think about any hindrances that may be holding you back from fully running the race marked out for you. Ask the Holy Spirit to reveal how you can "let go" and "go forth."

If you are in a time of grieving, meditate on the passages in Isaiah 26:3 and 61:3. As a decree in prayer, thank the Lord for His promise to keep you in perfect peace as you keep your mind on Him, and for giving you beauty for ashes and the garments of praise for a spirit of heaviness.

Prayer of Declaration

> *Heavenly Father, in accordance with Your Word, I declare that I will run the race You have marked out before me with passion and determination. Thank You for the gift of a season of grieving, in which I can honor my dear one and begin the healing process, and also for the ability to release the past and move forward as You lead.*
> *In the name of Jesus, I pray. Amen.*

Resources for Growing in Christ

- Many Scripture references in this book (noted with TPT) are taken from one of my all-time favorite translations of the Bible: The Passion Translation.
- YouVersion is a free Bible app with access to numerous translations.
- Patricia King Ministries is another personal favorite, especially her teachings and books on Decreeing God's Word. Also, be sure to check out her Web Church through Shiloh Fellowship—a great option for caregivers and others who, for various reasons, are not able to attend a local fellowship.
- Andrew Wommack Ministries offers an extensive volume of free content online, including resources you may find particularly helpful if you are a new believer. Their Helpline, (719) 635-1111, is staffed by prayer ministers 24/7 to answer questions and pray for any needs.

Notes

Day 4—Your Divine Teacher and Encourager

1. Our Daily Bread, The Power in Meekness by C.P. Hia, July 24, 2008. https://odb.org/US/2008/07/24/the-power-in-meekness

Day 5—With Him, All Things Are Possible

1. 1 Peter 2:24
2. Spafford, Horatio G., and Philip P. Bliss. 1873. *It Is Well With My Soul*. Ira Sankey.

Day 8—His Command to Love

1. Commentary on John 15:13, The Passion Translation: Or "willingly lay down his soul for his friends." The Aramaic word for "friends" is actually "family" or "relatives."

Day 12—Faith That Pleases God

1. Worship leader, author, and songwriter, Julie Meyer offers insightful and inspirational teaching on singing the Scriptures and has written a book on the subject, *Singing the Scriptures: How All Believers Can Experience Breakthrough, Hope and Healing,* that you may find helpful.

Day 13—Your Words Declare

1. King, Patricia. 2020. *The Power of the Decree*, pp.30-31. Bloomington, MN: Chosen Books.

Day 21—Divine Health

1. Satan tried to tempt Jesus when He was in the wilderness. Note how Jesus used Scripture, quoting it in answer to the accuser (Matthew 4:1–11).
2. For more information on healing, visit Andrew Wommack Ministries' Healing Center online: https://www.awmi.net/healing/

Day 22—Sowing and Reaping

1. Jerry Savelle, Calling in Your Harvest #1: https://www.youtube.com/watch?v=WXXGQz-rZy4&t=1256s

Day 27—Gaze Upon Him and Shine

1. 'Gaither Gospel Series: Bill Gaither Presents A Gospel Bluegrass Homecoming.' Gaither Music TV/YouTube. July 23, 2012. Video, https://www.youtube.com/playlist?list=OLAK5uy_kW2MCS06LjI-UWPTezkDpR4JKKYpu34V8Q.
2. 'Marty Stuart & His Fabulous Superlatives - This Little Light of Mine [Live].' Gaither Music TV/YouTube. July 23, 2012. Video, https://www.youtube.com/watch?v=_RZ-IjzkUss.

Day 28—Reflect the Fruit of the Spirit

1. I've chosen names to reflect what these caregivers meant to me and/or attributes of the fruit, rather than their given names. In total, there were about fifty individuals who helped us, all dearly appreciated!

Day 30—Walking Homeward

1. 'Jim Hill - What a Day That Will Be [Live].' Gaither Music TV/YouTube. September 10, 2012. Video, https://www.youtube.com/watch?v=SnvZL_zW2JI.

Acknowledgments

First and foremost, I am exceptionally grateful to the Lord for entrusting me with this devotional book to share. May His blessing be upon it to bear abundant fruit for His Kingdom.

Heartfelt thanks to so many dear family members and friends, caregivers, and pastors who prayed for, helped, and encouraged me through my caregiving years and my writing process. You have each been a special gift to me from the Lord. May He richly reward you for your kindness!

I would like to express my sincere personal appreciation to Jeremiah and Teresa Yancy and their Messenger publishing team, including our mentors and coaches, Dr. Brian Simmons, Patricia King, Rebecca Greenwood, and David Sluka. Many thanks to each of you and the entire team for your inspirational guidance, support, and prayers. I owe you a great debt of gratitude for enabling me to Unlock My Book, and especially for helping me to embrace The Messenger Life.

Letter from the Author

Dear Reader,

Thank you for taking the time to read my devotional!

During my caregiving days, I loved reading books written by caregivers—I felt a special connection with the authors, who seemed to uniquely empathize with what I was going through. Their words were soothing, and provided the practical, emotional, and spiritual support I needed. May my story, woven together with Scripture, be a blessing to strengthen and encourage you in your own journey.

As I have shared, I believe the Lord prepared me to Keep Mother at home, though my vision for my life had not included that season. But when the time came in which Mother needed my help, I knew that I knew...I was called to the role of her caregiver. Though I admittedly battled misgivings, I never wavered in my conviction that I was fulfilling the purpose the Lord had for me at that time. That assurance helped me persist when my feelings of physical and emotional weariness were convincingly signaling, "I can't do this anymore!"

I've also tried to be candid about my frustrations and struggles through the years, along with the grace of God (and my mother's forgiving nature) that completely overshadowed my every failing. I believe that most caregivers desire to serve their loved one well, and yet struggle under the enormity of the task. While my own strength and abilities could not enable me to perfectly care for Mother with patience and a joyful countenance all of the time, I understood that my key to success was in maintaining an attitude of humility, seeking forgiveness when I fell short, and in all circumstances, drawing near to the Lord.

So, my desire in writing this book has been to inspire you—take courage, and follow God's leading. In every season of life, you can trust Him to be faithful to His promises. In Him is—and always will be—wisdom for your every decision, with the sufficiency and provision for your every need.

Praying for you and cheering you on,

Darlene

About the Author

Darlene Goodwin began her writing career while serving as a naval officer, having enjoyed the privilege of crafting speeches, congressional testimony, and other written material for flag officers and senior executives, including the secretary of the navy. Following her retirement from active duty, she continued her service with the navy in civilian roles in public affairs and speechwriting.

Like many family caregivers, Darlene brought her elderly mother home when she became unable to live independently. Several years later, Darlene chose to bring her career to a close to focus more fully on her mother's care.

For a total of eleven years, with no previous experience or training in medical or dementia care, Darlene kept her mother at home through the increasingly challenging and exhausting progression of dementia and cancer. With support from a dedicated team of caregivers, doctors and nurses, hospice staff, chaplains, friends, and neighbors, Darlene was able to grant her mother's heartfelt desire to live at home until she transitioned to her heavenly home.

Caregiving was an unexpected and life-transforming journey for Darlene, leading her to dream of one day writing a book to encourage other family caregivers and those considering keeping a loved one—the devotional you now read. Darlene loves reading inspirational books, writing to inspire, and declaring Bible verses in word and song. She lives in her sunny home state of Florida, while holding a special place in her heart for her beloved Arizona.

Made in the USA
Columbia, SC
04 March 2025

a10ac875-fcb8-409d-805b-57c5759a6730R01